HOW TO BOUNCE BACK WITH

A RENEWED KICK-ASS APPROACH

EMILY HURLEY-WILKINSON

Copyright © Emily Hurley-Wilkinson 2017

Emily Hurley-Wilkinson has asserted her right under the Copyright, Designs and Patent Act 1988 to be identified as the author of this work.

This book is sold subject to the condition it shall not, by way of trade or otherwise, be circulated in any form or by any means, electronic or otherwise without the author's prior consent.

Every effort has been made, to reference copyright material, both illustrative and quoted.

ISBN 978-1976483127

Note to Readers

This book carries the opinions and ideas of the author. It is intended to provide helpful and informative material on a variety of subjects contained within the book. As each reader's situation is unique, the content of this book is general and its purpose is to provide general information rather than address any medical, psychological, nutritional or any other kind of professional therapy.

The author disclaims all responsibility for any liability, loss or risk, personal or otherwise, which is incurred as a consequence, directly or indirectly, of the use and application of any of the contents in this book.

Dedication

In memory of my Dad, who sadly passed away during the writing of this book; an eloquent story teller with many a tale to share and who often joked about writing his own book one day.

And for my mum, who along with Dad taught me the true value of life - 'that the most important things in life aren't things.'

Because of you both, my life is blessed in many wonderful ways.

Acknowledgements

During the writing of this book I experienced a mixed bag of emotions; from frustration and self-doubt, to feelings of deep pleasure and satisfaction. During these past few years there has been enormous upheaval, confusion, fear and heartache, yet through all this chaos and sorrow, writing this book has had a very stabilising effect on me - in many ways it has been my anchor.

Bringing this book to life was a big undertaking, and I would not have completed this goal without the unwavering support of my husband Spencer, my rock and for whom without, my life would be incomplete - because of your belief in me, I have achieved a dream. To my two amazing sons Josh and Ben, without your patience, support and sense of humour, this book would have been an even greater challenge. I am proud of you both beyond measure.

To my sisters Linda and Liz, for all the tears, laughter and crazy moments shared together. Especially to you Linda, for being such a guiding light as I wrote this book, and always ready to kick my ass when it needed kicking.

To a dear friend, and highly proficient international business journalist, Pepi Sappal, thank you from the bottom of my heart for your guidance, words of encouragement and for proof reading – I never realised how fond I was of exclamation marks!

Chris Atkinson, an inspirational business speaker, thank you for your honest feedback and advice. Sincere thanks to Robert Smith, of Robert Smith Literary Agency Ltd. for your time and feedback. It was great getting to know you.

A heart-felt thanks to my nephew Cian Twomey for capturing the cover pictures, and for your support and advice on social media development.

To my brothers Dave, Darren and Stephen at Prisma Print Ltd. for taking on the challenge of printing the book – that was a big endeavour, and one for which I am enormously grateful.

And to my friends, colleagues and clients who have been a part of my life, in differing ways you have all been an inspiration.

Finally, to you my dear friends, Kate and Adrian, thank you for your love and support especially during those difficult times.

CONTENTS

ACKNOWLEDGEMENTS..VII
WHY THIS BOOK MATTERS..XI
INTRODUCTION XIII

PART I - GET UNSTUCK

1 GET OUT OF YOUR OWN WAY..19
2 HOW TO INCREASE SELF-BELIEF 33
3 DEVELOP EMOTIONAL SELF-DISCIPLINE........................51

PART II - STOP EMOTIONAL REACTIVITY

4 INTRODUCING SYSTEM PAUSE..61

PART III - FIVE BEST WAYS TO BOUNCE BACK

5 THE POWER & SCIENCE OF POSITIVITY 73
6 ACCEPTANCE - FINDING INNER PEACE 91
7 DEVELOPING A 'CAN DO' ATTITUDE 101
8 HELP YOURSELF - THE 360° LIFE MAKE-OVER............119
9 USING EMPATHY FOR BETTER RELATIONSHIPS........155

CASE STUDIES 171
AFTERWORD..177
RECLAIM YOUR MOJO - THE A-Z GUIDE 179
REFERENCES 185

x

Why This Book Matters

We are all guilty of being self-doubters to the point where we become passive, we then settle for less no longer expecting more for ourselves or of ourselves. And with each passing year our sparkle dims as we encounter one too many experiences that shakes the basis of our self-worth. In my personal and professional life, I see too many people living like this to the point where they become stuck, stressed out and resentful of their circumstances.

My purpose in writing this book is to inspire and empower you to get back to the business of living, by taking charge of your life once and for all. You will learn how to bounce back from difficulties with a renewed kick-ass approach.

I share with you key life skills that guide you through in detail, how to immediately turn on the brain's calm switch, five essential characteristics essential for developing emotional resilience, along with many practical and refreshingly simple exercises, designed to help you get unstuck and back on the recovery road to a more confident, visible and happier you.

I am no stranger to adversity and have been through an extraordinary amount of difficulties so far. This book includes many of these personal stories, so that you get to understand that life side swipes all of us in various ways, but you do have a choice in how you react. And this, dear reader, is why this book matters.

As you begin to feel empowered and inspired, your confidence will emerge, and you will begin to move forwards with the people and things that really matter the most.

Are you ready to bounce back and kick-ass? Let's Get Your Mojo Back!

Introduction

IS THIS IT? Is this me? I look in the mirror and barely notice the person staring back. A tired and disillusioned face etched with mistakes, regrets and a sinking feeling that it might be too late to claw back lost dreams and hopes. "Life used to be simple and uncomplicated. I felt alive and full of hope".

This by far is one of the most common stories that I hear from all kinds of people who come to me for personal coaching. And I get it. As a working mum of two boys, I have had my own share of mirror moments during my life that shook my world, as I felt my own Mojo heading for a meltdown.

Over the past few years, my life has been full of uncertainty, confusion and too much stress. Having fled my structurally damaged home, due to a catalogue of ill health, meant I endured four home moves in just five years. The net effect of that, meant I had to navigate my way through seven years of the legal system, negotiate with a bank whose only goal was repossession of this structurally damaged home, and manoeuvre my way through an overpriced rental market, where available houses were in short supply.

Add to that, the theft of my business identity, which brought undercover officials to my door, several health scares, which saw me in the hospital theatre one too many times, along with the death of my Dad, who lost his life in what became a very traumatic and bizarre experience.

That was in addition to other previous mirror moments encountered along the way, when I decided to push the reset button of my life, and move country, largely motivated by finding my then partner of many years, in bed with another woman.

All of which left me feeling derailed, depleted, emotionally overwhelmed, and in serious search of my Mojo!

So I do get it, I do understand that sinking feeling of self-doubt and frustration, where you just know there is more to you than the face staring back at you in the mirror.

My Story

Born in Ireland, I became interested in 'people development' shortly after leaving school. It didn't take long before I got a job working as a personal assistant for a model agency. The experience was a colourful one, and taught me that despite the physical beauty of the people I met along the way, many were living with low self-esteem. I was trained to teach people how to convey confidence through their demeanour and image, which I found fascinating, rewarding and fun. Though, I was to later understand that these two techniques alone were just the tip of the iceberg.

In the late '90s, with my mojo full to the brim and my self-belief clocking in at the higher end of the continuum scale, I set off to London to follow a dream. The years that followed saw me graft my way to senior management within the harsh environment of media, working for several reputable international media corporations before I finally turned my hand at developing my own sales training company. My interest in 'people development' grew stronger, as did my hunger for all things 'self development'.

In 2002 I returned to Ireland, and some few years later became an accredited Personal/Business Coach and achieved certification in rational emotive behavioural therapy. Cognitive behavioural coaching is my passion and as a result, some know me as a Mind Coach. Without the labels, in simple terms, I am a person who helps people to help themselves.

Life only happens once, and I believe that people deserve to live their best life. All too often we lose our way, and we lose our sense of self as we morph into the multiple roles that life demands, often at the cost of our own needs and happiness.

Throughout my journey so far, I have met with the most thrilling, beautiful and breath-taking experiences and equally, I have had an extraordinary amount of stomach wrenching, heart breaking and jaw dropping encounters. But it was in those dark moments of anguish, that my best lessons were learned.

PART I

GET UNSTUCK

Chapter 1

Get Out of Your Own Way

> 'The tragedy of life is not that it ends so soon, but that we wait so long to begin it'[1]

"Can I really change my life or is it too late?" I am often asked this question and I usually reply by reminding those that ask that they have two choices; to accept their life and current circumstances as it is now and to stop groaning and get on with it, or to accept responsibility for changing it and lose the excuses.

When I made the decision to pack my life into yet another suitcase and make the long haul flight from Australia to England, having spent that year living as a lady of leisure, I was terrified by going it alone. Many people looking from the outside in thought I had it all, the champagne lifestyle, the stable relationship, plush apartment overlooking the beach, luxury car, exotic holidays, yet surrounded by all this glitz and glamour, I never felt more alone.

I was soul starved, with a realization that I was not living my dream but that of someone else. I had a gnawing feeling that I was selling myself short, only existing in a relationship where a differing of values became more obvious as each day passed.

I remember thinking at the time, "It's too late to change now. How can I start again on my own? Where would I go, how would I support myself, I can't live on my own in a faceless big city such as London, can I?"

My mind swirled with fear and self-doubt with so many questions unanswered in the face of uncertainty. So I quickly withdrew to my comfort zone, where excuses became my best defence. "Maybe it's best to wait… I'll wait until I have more courage or feel more certain about this. I'll wait to see if things change."

Like wildfire, excuses were rampant in my mind as I desperately tried to blind myself to the naked truth. Either I accept things as they are, despite the pain and disappointments that came with that or I 'Reclaim my Mojo' and start living on my terms.

I knew I was not ready for a return to my hometown of Ireland. I just could not visualise myself back in my old bedroom with a rabbit and hamster for room-mates, living on sympathy and tea with my parents - wonderful, loving and supportive as they were. Deep down my inner voice kept nudging me to be true to myself, that the best of me was yet to be realised.

Even though I had no idea where I was going, nor how I would re-start, I pushed myself to step out of my comfort zone and step up to the edge of the unknown to set off in search of new beginnings. I see too many people living their lives passively as if their entire life is determined by their current circumstances.

The fact is that when you live your life with that mindset, it allows you to deny responsibility for your own happiness and wellbeing. We are not always in control of what life throws at us, this I know, but we are always in control of how we react and of the choices that we make.

A question I often ask people who wonder if it might be too late is this, "If today was the last day of your life, what would be your biggest regret?" Then the floodgates open: "I regret spending so much time worrying about what others thought of me, I regret worrying about things that never happened, I regret not leaving my unfulfilling relationship, I regret staying in my job, I regret not taking more risks, I regret not seeing more of the world, I regret not being more active, I regret not facing the truth, I regret not being more responsible, I regret not being more patient and loving,

I regret not trying, I regret not spending more time with my kids, or parents", and so on.

The point here is this - the underlying regret here is about change and taking a chance. People regret not using courage to become more and do more. The next time you catch yourself wishing things were different within your life, pay attention to the amount of excuses that roll off your tongue.

Over the years how many times have you said any of the following? "If only I had more time, more money, more energy, more courage, more confidence, more information, more certainty, more positivity, less stress, less pain, less weight," etc. Whatever it is, you just wanted more or less of it before you got started.

Never underestimate the human capacity for self-deception. Each year large sums of money get spent by thousands of people looking for ways to become more visible and to live happier, more meaningful lives. In many cases, these solutions are short cuts, avoidance techniques and excuse trips.

All too often I see people give up, no longer expecting more from themselves. Paralysed by self-imposed fears and self-doubts they remain resentful of their circumstances, relationships or lifestyle, yet they carry on regardless, despite the pain or feelings of unhappiness. They might convince themselves that things will be different next year or maybe they may even receive a windfall.

What excuses have you created to make your life more bearable?

The first few years of my journey to reclaim my mojo was by no means an easy one. In search of my new path brought with it, lashings of nail-biting, stomach-wrenching and heart-thumping moments. On returning to London from Australia, my first priority was to find a job to support myself and a place to live. For the first few months I stayed on the floor on a blow up mattress in a flat of my two dear friends Kate and Adrian, whose support, encouragement and belief in me helped push me through many challenging and dark days.

I recall one day in particular as I routinely battled my way down the steps of an over-crowed train station, when my mobile rang. It was Kate, whose living room floor I had set up camp in. She had called to check in on me. Her words of support touched me that day, as she told me how she likened me to the mythical bird, The Phoenix. "You have soared to great heights often defying the odds Emily, and I just know you will rise again as a stronger, wiser version of you."

That day, Kate's words acted as a reminder of what I already knew deep down - that the best of me was yet to come, so long as I was committed to soaring to new heights. Having previously worked for Maxwell Consumer Publishing, a well-known international media sales corporation in London, as head of department managing several sales staff, I felt hopeful that my return to work in London would be a gentle transition. Instead I was offered a job at yet another highly reputable international media corporation, News International. Only this time working as a junior telesales executive, whose motto was 'You are only as good as you last sale'. As grateful as I was for securing employment, in terms of career, I was transported several years back in time, back on the first step of the ladder and needing to prove my professional sales ability all over again.

The hard slog of media sales and the veil of loneliness began to fray on my already tattered nerves. I spent many days and nights mulling things over, twisting things around in my head, questioning repeatedly all the 'whys', 'what ifs' and 'if only'. There were many times when returning to my old bedroom in Ireland with Mocha, the rabbit and Hammy, the hamster seemed like the sensible choice.

Weekends were particularly tough in London for a single girl without single friends and being single in a coupled world does have its limitations. In fact, I used to look forward to Mondays, going back to the hard slog of sales, just to escape the loneliness.

With a bottle of wine, The Jerry Springer show and Celine Dion's rendition of 'All By Myself' as my main source of comfort and entertainment, (cliché I know, but very much my reality at that time), I knew I had to get off the gravy train of self-pity, lose the excuses and get out of my own way.

It was time for an emotional detox and a life makeover.

I began to journal my thoughts in order to make sense of them. On doing so, one thing became very clear to me; that my choices from now on must reflect my hopes and dreams, and not my fears[17]. I realised that when uncertainty is the only certainty[2], its' precisely at these moments in life that you're true potential is revealed to you if you are willing to give yourself a chance to see it.

Pinned to my mirror I placed the words: 'It does not matter where you are today - what does matter is where you are going.'[18] Within a relatively short period of time, I found an apartment outside of London, and I began to climb the professional ladder securing a promotion at work.

Trust me when I say that before you can create your future, you must first accept where you are right now and believe that whatever it is you want to achieve, you already have all that it takes to set this process in motion.

There will never be a right time to make changes and if you are honest with yourself, you already know this at some level. The fact is that as long as you stand in your own way with a mind brimming with all the reasons why you can't, you will remain stuck.

You're Best Life Starts Here

Before you get started, consider this.

- You must make an emotional commitment and be willing to experience discomfort as you move from your comfort zone of predictable habits.

- You must be willing to acknowledge that real change is not a quick-fix solution.

- You must be willing to cut yourself some slack and accept that no matter what side swipes you in your journey of change, you are capable of moving through it, as tough as that might be at times.

It is important that you get clear about what it is that you want, and <u>not</u> what you think others want of you. What you are capable of achieving, must not be as a result of what others think is possible or not possible for you.

Think about what is true for you and why it is important to you, and what <u>not</u> achieving it will mean for you.

You may have to face some truths about yourself, and push yourself in a direction that may seem uncomfortable or even scary. But know that if that is the case, you can enlist the help of friends or professionals. Keep it simple too. So many people make the mistake that only big and radical change will make a difference. Let's not forget the old adage that 'A journey of a thousand miles starts with one single step.'[19]

Know that when you start to make progress, you will feel a sense of achievement, which in turn will help you to feel more visible as your self confidence will start to re-emerge. Get a glimpse of your future now with the following exercise.

Exercise - The Magic Mirror

Imagine being granted an opportunity to get a glimpse of what your future holds. Let's try a fun exercise that will give you that opportunity. All you need is your imagination and a pen and paper to jot down any thoughts that follow.

Just for now, I would like for you to imagine standing in front of a full length mirror. Now imagine walking through this magic mirror, and when you reach the other side you realise that the mirror has brought you exactly five years into your future. It is exactly five years from today.

Try it now, stop and vividly imagine it.

Grab a pen, and use the checklist opposite.

Notice what's different, what has changed within you and outside of you?

- How are you different?

- Who and what do you see around you?

- Notice how your attitude and behaviour has changed? What do you notice about your demeanour? Notice any changes in the way you now walk and hold yourself?

- Notice the sort of things you now say to yourself about your life and self.

- What do you hear other people saying about you?

- How do you feel? Have you ever felt that feeling before?

- Is the picture of your future five years from now positive?

- Is your reflection one that makes you fulfilled and alive?

- How have you grown and evolved?

- In what ways are you now enjoying life and new experiences?

- How does this picture compare to your current life?

- Conversely, did your picture capture an older version of you repeatedly doing all that you've done before?

Make some notes

Do not underestimate the power of this exercise as it helps you to create a vision for your life. When you hold a clear and vivid picture of how you want your life to be, you are simply declaring what it is that you want to experience, what it is that you want to accomplish and the person you want to become.

In many ways, I believe that when you keep such a vision burning bright within your minds' eye, it will act as an invisible hand, that will guide you through times of self-doubt and fear as it did for me on many occasions.

If repeated often enough, this process becomes easier, and your vision for your future will become clearer, brighter and stronger. There are times when people find this exercise hard initially, as they have become so disillusioned by disappointments and failures. If that is the case for you, then understand this - when a dream that was can no longer be (for whatever reason), then it is time to dream a different dream.

Never allow your current circumstances dictate your future, because you are worth more. The following extract on the page overleaf, is an example of the inner strength and courage within us all, if we are willing to venture beyond the shackles of our fears and self-doubts.

It's about risk and trust and the magic that can happen when you allow yourself to believe in better.

"Come to the edge," he said.

"We're comfortable back here," they said.

"Come to the edge," he said.

"We're too busy," they said.

"Come to the edge," he said. "It's too high," they said.

"Come to the edge," he said.

"We're afraid," they said.

"Come to the edge," he said.

"We'll fall," they said.

"Come to the edge," he said.

And they did.

And he pushed them.

And they flew.

Christopher Logue

Now think how long you have stood at the edge of your life waiting for a push? Remember, the only point at which you can change things is today - yesterday is a memory and tomorrow is just a thought.

Chapter 2

How to Increase Self-Belief

> '**Only as high as I reach, can I grow.**
>
> **Only as far as I seek, can I go.**
>
> **Only as deep as I look, can I see.**
>
> **Only as much as I dream, can I be.**'[3]

Throughout my life I have had many people telling me how they wished that they had confidence like me. Initially, I found this fascinating. I questioned why so many people perceived me, as being confident, as I too had wrestled with issues of confidence. I know what it feels like to want to shy away from voicing an opinion, for fear of sounding stupid or inadequate in some way.

I know what it feels like to feel paralysed by fear when giving a talk or presentation, in case I was not received well. I know what it feels like to not feel pretty enough, intelligent enough or just good enough at certain things. Yet in spite of these insecurities, people continued to admire my confidence. Why? How is it that, others saw confidence ooze from me, when I felt otherwise?

I believe it comes down to three key factors that are intertwined – Courage, Self-Concept and Body Talk. Despite my fears and these feelings of not been 'enough', I took positive action. I mustered up the courage to act instead of reacting or shy away, and I did not allow self-doubt to entirely rule my mind. In spite of my fears and doubts, I took action. I became proactive rather than reactive.

Courage – In a nutshell, courage is defined as a state of mind that enables us to face change, uncertainty and fear. I know that courage is deeply rooted within us all; it is not something that we are born with or without. Within the first chapter you may recall me writing:

'I realised that when uncertainty is the only certainty, that it is precisely at these moments in life that your true potential is revealed to you, if you are willing to give yourself a chance to see it.'

That is what I mean by courage.

Courage is always there within you and life will continue to provide you with many opportunities to use it. When you choose to let courage emerge by taking action, regardless of how small this action is, it is then that you will sow the seeds of confidence and self-belief.

I have had to call on courage on countless occasions throughout my journey. One of my earliest memories was my first job interview in London on first moving to the UK from Ireland.

The newspaper advertisement had read something along the lines of 'Professional sales people required for the launch of a quality national broadsheet newspaper based in London. Graduates need only apply, sales experience preferable.'

Needless to say that my sales experience was limited to that of a brief time in retail sales in a small designer boutique in my hometown of Ireland, and in terms of qualifications, I graduated from the University of Life. With my more to gain and little to lose mindset, I called the company and assured them that I was worth an interview at the very least. As I sat in the plush London office, feeling intimidated by the thoughts of being interrogated, I caught my reflection in the mirror. Slumped in the oversized sofa did not make for a great impression. I quickly adjusted my posture. I recall feeling terrified and apprehensive as there was a clear deficit in my skills and qualifications in relation to their needs.

Despite the shadow of doubt that had descended on me, there and then, I called on courage and reminded myself of my personal strengths and qualities. I also brought to mind the value that I could bring to them based on my personal qualities. Within a couple of minutes, I felt more assured and ready to showcase brand 'Emily'. The interview was a success and as a result of sheer courage, I achieved my first big break in the media industry in London.

Now think of something that you would love to do or try but have avoided doing as a result of fear and feeling inadequate in some way. Become aware of the quality of your thinking and make some notes.

Remember courage is a state of mind. It is vital that you understand that being courageous does not mean <u>not</u> being afraid, it does not mean that you suddenly stop having self-doubts. What it does mean, is doing things <u>despite</u> those fears and doubts. Often when we think we lack courage, it is a screen for not wanting to experience emotional pain, frustration or failure, and if you are honest with yourself, you will begin to acknowledge this fact too.

As a result we use avoidance as a way of coping, which is by far a very poor long-term solution. Ironically, not only does avoidance make fears stronger, but it leads to a cascade of negative feelings including guilt, regret, anger and anxiety, not to mention the many missed opportunities as a result of avoidance. Had I not called that company when I did, I would never had met the many amazing people I encountered back then, nor gained invaluable experience.

A great way to help you to get clear on your strengths and qualities is to do a personal strengths inventory or as I like to call a PSI. By knowing your strengths, you can focus your efforts on the things that you are good at, and uncover what sets you apart from other people.

When thinking about your strengths, don't limit yourself to just education or work skills. Think of your personality traits, personal achievements and interests too.

To help you get started, you might want to consider the following questions:

Personal Strengths Inventory

- What do you get recognised or complimented for?

- What are your achievements and can you reframe them as strengths?

- What are you really good at and feels effortless?

- What are you most proud of about yourself?

- What do you do better than other people you know?

- Where do you see the most potential for yourself and why?

- What things would you love to try or do but have avoided so far?

Self-Concept – This is no different, for it too fundamentally is a state of mind. Simply put, self-concept is how you perceive yourself, the stories that you tell yourself, which are a reflection of all your life experiences. Once you understand, that it is your experiences that have shaped your thinking and attitudes, you will understand that your thoughts about who you are, are just that - thoughts. Once you acknowledge and accept that, you become free to change and grow.

If your thoughts bring you down or hold you back in some way, then it's time to think differently in order to experience life differently. What you believe about yourself can blind you from the truth of who you really are and of what's possible. You can either become a victim of your own thinking and as a result get stuck, or you can become a victor of your life, having the courage of your convictions to feel and experience more.

From my own experience, it seems that we all have developed negative and critical ways of seeing ourselves. Indeed I have spent years coaching people through all sorts of issues and truthfully what has stood in their way has not been so much about who 'they are' but who they think 'they are not'.

"I don't have enough confidence or charm, I'm not tall, smart, assertive, talkative or experienced enough; basically not enough" Of course, when we feel we lack in some way, we are quick to stamp a label on our identity. As a result, a life debilitating condition that I call 'Ican'titis' (I can't itis)' develops. 'Itis' is a term usually used with reference to a disease, and in this instance I use it with reference to a state of mind that is compared to a disease, for I believe too many people are caught up in this loop of belittling and undervaluing themselves. All efforts to become more are sabotaged by 'Ican'titis'.

Can you recall when you were a child all the things you dreamt of being and doing? Think about that now, perhaps you thought about being a dentist, nurse, teacher, business owner, lecturer, scientist, dancer, politician, actor, writer, rally driver, presenter, singer, photographer, entertainer or any other occupation or dream your mind conceived of. Your mind was full of possibilities, opportunities and dreams. What about today?

How do you see yourself now?

What has changed from your previous years? Do you now only see all the reasons why it's not possible, why you can't? Have you become a victim of 'Ican'titis' – a victim of your own thinking?

You cannot touch the wind, but you can feel its effect. Your thoughts are no different. It's astounding the level of power that your mind can have over you and ultimately the way you live your life. What you believe about yourself can enrich your life and bring you great happiness and fulfilment, or it can drag you down and bring you sadness, anger, anxiety and a life full of bitterness and regret.

As we journey through life from childhood to adulthood, what we think and believe about ourselves changes and not always for the better. Sadly, we begin to buy into other people's opinions and beliefs about who we are and what we are capable of, and accept these ideas as fact without ever disputing or changing them. Stuff happens and none of us are immune from this stuff, because this stuff is called life. And whilst our experiences can cloud our view of ourselves and of life in general, we do not have to allow these experiences to define us. If we continue to be defined by experiences and by others' opinions, the outcome will be that we only ever truly know other people's versions of who we are.

The net effect is that we become stifled by insecurities and self-doubts and so fail to fully understand who we can be and what we are truly capable of. As children we believe what we're told about ourselves; as adults we carry on telling ourselves these same messages never refuting them.

It is said that elephants in captivity are trained at an early age, not to roam; one leg of a baby elephant is tied with a rope to a small wooden post planted in the ground. Initially the baby elephant tries to break free from the rope, but the rope is too strong.

The baby elephant learns - and believes - that it can't break the rope. When the elephant grows up and is mighty, it could easily break the same rope. But because it learned that it couldn't break the rope when it was young, the adult elephant 'believes' that it still can't break the rope, so it doesn't even try.

People are no different. When we learn something about ourselves at an early age, we tend to still believe it as an adult. Even though it may not be true for us today, we function as if it is. When you tried something new and your expected outcome was disappointing, were you told you'd never be good at it or were your efforts the source of humour for others? Maybe you excelled at something and through the eyes of another's envy you were labelled a show off.

Perhaps you can recall your parents unwittingly label you as the shy one of the family. All too often teachers, parents, friends are quick to affix a name on us as if it was part of our identity. "He is the clever one, she is the timid one, he is a loner, the one who is not good with people, computers, sports," and so on. We passively accept these labels as part of our self-concept and allow them to become part of our identity.

Many of us would have encountered a teacher at some point in our schooling, who just seemed highly critical of us. I talk about teachers because like our parents, these people have enormous influence on our children, and can impact on our self-concept in unimaginable ways. Just one stressed-out, judgemental or hard to please teacher can often trigger a reaction of life-long insecurities, self-doubt and fear of failure – if we allow it to.

I recall having my nose pulled by a teacher, who asked with rhetoric "Are you stupid" – because I had failed to read an extract from a book based on her expectations, about how I should have read it. I was in junior school.

At the time, I thought I must be stupid, if this teacher - a trusted person in authority - believes I am. Ironically, "Don't be so smart," was often her response to me, when I tried to explain myself further.

Because of her intimidating manner, I used to try to fly under the radar in fear of being singled out. As a result a good day in class was when I remained invisible. There were many occasions when I felt my heart beat so hard, I thought I would pass out.

I have no doubt that there are many schools and teachers that now promote and support a holistic learning approach. However, I also wonder how many teachers continue to label students based on their own limited views. I wonder what percent of teachers continue to use fear as a prime motivator? How many of our students still fear making mistakes, fear speaking out of turn or speaking up in the case of being wrongly accused of a misdemeanour? It would seem that this approach unintentionally lowers our children's self-esteem, to conform and comply with outdated learning approaches.

What kinds of things did your teachers, parents, friends, boyfriends, partners and others around you tell you as you aged? What were you encouraged to do, say and be, and discouraged from doing and being? How often did you hear people say that certain things that you believed possible aren't possible, or that you aren't good enough, smart enough, tall enough, fast enough, confident enough etc?

More often than not it would seem that labels follow us throughout our lives. Many things that we were told as a child and young teenager stick with us our entire lives and shape how we perceive ourselves today. Many messages are positive, encouraging and life supporting, however several are negative, life draining and erode away at our self-esteem.

Well enough is enough - it's time you seek the truth of your potential.

The Truth – You are not always the stories that you tell yourself, you are not the sum of your experiences and you are not always what you believe. By continuing to let your past define who you are, you disconnect from the person you really are. By continuing to live your life through old, worn-out self-sabotaging beliefs and thoughts, life will continue to be difficult and unfulfilling for you.

As a result you may never make the right choices, or take the necessary action towards living a more enriching life.

Do you remember 'The Wizard of Oz?' The Wizard turns out to be just an ordinary man behind the curtain; not a great wizard as many had thought. When his real identity is unveiled, he explains to Dorothy and her friends that each of them already possesses all that they are searching for.

The 'Great Wizard' then gives each of them a gift to reinforce all that they were in search of. He pins a medal on the Lion as a symbol of courage, the Tin Man is presented with a watch in the shape of a heart that symbolise his emotions and to Scarecrow he gives a certificate to symbolise his intellect. As each accepts their gift from the 'Great Wizard' they become instantly transformed.

Why?

Because each gain a new belief about themselves!

Finally, the Good Witch of the North reminds Dorothy that: "You've always had the power to go back to Kansas" When Scarecrow asks the witch why she didn't tell Dorothy about this sooner, the Good Witch answers by saying, "because she would not have believed me." When Dorothy was asked what she had learned from her experience, she says,

"If I ever go looking for my heart's desire again, I won't look any further than my own backyard, because if it isn't there, I never lost it to begin with."

Self-belief was all that Dorothy and her friends needed to achieve their heart's desire. So whether you are in search of your 'Mojo' in order to feel more confident, alive and visible, more 'Courage' to make changes or to face life's challenges, more 'Heart' to have compassion or to be open to love, and more 'Intellect' to further your development - you have only to realise that you are 'enough' to bring about whatever your heart desires.

It does not matter how difficult you believe your situation is now, or how far out of reach you may think your dreams and aspirations are; the point is this - you can change your life by proactively doing something right now, today, to change it.

We all hold on to self-defeating ways of thinking and behaving, which is no longer a reflection of who we are now or who we want to become. If you are still waiting for a 'Great Wizard' to come and fix you and your life, the bottom line is that only you and you alone, have the power to instigate these changes.

Thought Journaling – 'You cannot change what you do not acknowledge'[20], is a well-established fact and true saying. The best way to get clear on negative and irrational thoughts is to listen to them. We rarely, if ever stop and dispute our thoughts, but by capturing them on paper, you automatically empower yourself to see things more clearly and rationally.

Begin by making daily entries to help you to work through your inner chatter.

The following exercise will help guide you.

Thought Journal

How often do you belittle yourself?

Are you critical of your appearance, your mind or abilities?

Do you put yourself down in front of others?

Do you stop yourself from doing or trying things you want to do because you think you won't be good at it, might fail, or embarrass yourself?

Do you stop yourself from trying things because there's always someone who's better than you?

Each day, pay deliberate attention and actively listen to your negative stories that you tell yourself, and write each one down within your journal. Start to question how valid they are. Get curious. Find out the origins of your inner critic.

Can you recall specific moments and experiences in your life that have impacted on how you see yourself, others and life today?

I remember coaching a man who was highly motivated to work on being more assertive, however what we learned during his consultation, was that embedded deep within his mind was a belief that he was born that way – passive, and found it hard to believe or imagine himself being anything else, let alone assertive. From the off, we had to work through getting rid of these ideas that he had about himself by replacing them with new experiences that led to new beliefs.

Remember, we are not born with negative thoughts – this enemy within makes itself known to us very early on, usually during early childhood, and over the years, this stealthy voice is accepted by ourselves as the voice of reason.

I truly believe that all of us would do more, try more and become more, if we got to know more about who we really are, instead of hiding behind our inner critic.

Body Talk – The Powerful Link between Posture and Mood

At some point during childhood, many of us would have been told to sit up straight and keep our chin up. Certainly during my era of schooling, I was encouraged to walk tall and with a spring in my step, on the many occasions that I walked home from school and passed Sister Eucharia, a refreshingly inspiring nun, and teacher who believed that posture was the gateway to happiness and wellbeing.

Did Sister Eucharia know back then what scientists reveal now?

We all know that when we are feeling sad, down or depressed there is a natural tendency for the body to move into a collapsed posture. Have you ever noticed your own posture or that of others when your mood is low? Our back becomes more rounded with dropped or hunched shoulders and our face is lowered towards the ground.

Conversely when we are feeling happy our posture is more upright and movement is more energised. This is an example of the relationship between mind and body. The connection between both is inextricably intertwined, an ancient philosophy, now accepted by science. Yet this undisputed fact is often overlooked by many of us.

In many ways, you could think of your body as an electrochemical factory. Because the language of your brain is chemical, it communicates with the rest of your body via these chemical compounds, therefore every thought you have and feeling you experience causes a reaction within your body. In fact, the chemical composition of your body is altered within seconds of one single thought.

Simply put, your body is responding continuously each day to how you think and feel.

So the deal is this, whatever way you are feeling every moment of every day, can either heal or hurt your body.

However, what if I told you, the relationship between the mind and body runs both ways. In other words, we know our posture is affected by our mood, but did you know that your mood is also altered by posture – this is a scientific fact.

Of the many available studies on this topic, a talk delivered by Professor Amy Cuddy of Harvard Business School shown on Ted Talks[4] is one of my favourite. Her very insightful and world renowned talk demonstrates how standing in a posture of confidence, for which she calls the 'power pose' can alter testosterone and cortisol levels in the body. It is suggested that levels of testosterone increase with an expansive posture, whilst levels of cortisol (stress hormone) decrease.

Indeed, across the animal kingdom, expansive postures are very notable, which is presumably representative of a 'power pose' for survival and hierarchy purposes. Notice the body language of animals the next time you come across a documentary about the wild. And you don't need to see animals in the wild for that matter. Expansive postures are also exhibited by many a successful person.

Amy Cuddy also reveals that not only can we change our own body's chemistry, but we can increase our own feelings of personal power and confidence levels, whilst at the same time shifting others perception of us by simply altering our body posture.

To be honest, this does not surprise me in the least, as I myself saw some amazing transformations during the years that I taught Deportment & Grooming in the early '90s. Girls that initially presented as shy or timid would appear and feel more self assured, energised and confident by simple adjustments to their posture.

Some reported feeling more visible and felt sexier, as they practiced better posture exercises between classes. In truth, when we feel more visible, we feel good, and when we feel good the benefits have a long-lasting ripple effect. One of the most valuable takeaways from Amy Cuddy's Ted Talk is this; in just two minutes of 'Power Poses' a day, you can change how you feel about yourself and subsequently how others perceive you.

It would seem Sister Eucharia was on point!

Given the amount of times people sit, whether at school, the car or the office, we have become a nation of slumpers, and worse still, we do very little if anything to rectify this, until it's too late and we find ourselves at the physiotherapist. If posture has been proven to be associated with higher self-esteem, better physical health and fewer negative emotions, surely then, it is time, that deportment/posture correction classes become part of the office, classroom and community at large.

50

Chapter 3

Develop Emotional Self-Discipline

> 'Emotions are not problems to be solved. They are signals to be interpreted.'[5]

I know too well, how easy it is to get swallowed up by emotional turmoil. Just when I thought I had the resilience of a 'water bear', (apparently the toughest animals on the planet because they can live happily under the most extreme conditions[6]), in 2014, I found myself under the surgeon's knife having a breast lumpectomy, having overcome pneumonia a year or so previously.

Yet, I would consider myself to be a generally positive, healthy and happy go lucky person. In terms of health, I was the girl that appeared in the local paper with the Lord Mayor of my city, receiving an award for having never being absent from school throughout my entire school years. However, I had begun to experience a great deal of emotional distress from the off on my relocation back to Ireland.

When I finally decided to make my comeback to my hometown, I returned eight months pregnant, along with my partner in tow, who was later to become my husband. The years that followed sent us on an emotional rollercoaster of highs and lows. Our first night brought us the tragic and life altering news from New Zealand, that my husband's father had passed away unexpectedly and tragically. Numb with shock and disorientated with confusion, we muddled along and some weeks later we became proud parents to our first child.

Though blessed with all the magic that parenthood can bring, it was a year of utter turbulence and chaos that saw us homeless for a time, where we lived out of a suitcase, sharing my sister's house during the day and my parent's home at night.

Caught up in a survival mentality can do one of two things to a person. It can lure you into a state of powerlessness and helplessness, or it can make you enterprising, resourceful and even more determined to reach your dreams. Because we both had a strong inner resilience, we remained undeterred, and so we etched out a path that saw us buy our dream family home, and we were blessed with another son.

Just one year after, having bagged what we thought was our dream home, cracks began to appear. I'm talking real physical enormous crevices in the entire house structure. Dark, black dangerous mould grew rampantly throughout as a result, and the rooms began to smell of the most awful unexplained putrid smell. Floor tiles became unstable and the house was excessively damp. Due to the severity of the cracking, we were sitting targets for a range of environmental toxins that would make their way through the cracks, not to mention, the poisons wafting throughout the house as a result of the uncontrollable mould.

When my eldest son was treated as an emergency patient for sudden acute asthma, with no previous history of respiratory difficulties, my concern around the dangers of our home environment began to increase. Those concerns were further compounded when my youngest son also developed respiratory difficulties, and ended up at the accident and emergency rooms when a radiator collapsed on him, and I went on to develop pneumonia.

We fled our home, scared out of our wits, feeling deeply confused, stressed, angry and hurt. The world economy began to tumble, and Ireland was in a financial melt-down, with many landlords abandoning their properties and absconding from Ireland.

As a result, renting during these unstable economic times, resulted in us moving home four times in a short period of time, (eleven home relocations since our return to Ireland, which is the equivalent of moving home every one and half years) and a bank in hot pursuit of us for their pound of flesh, despite them being fully made aware of the structural damage, and the pending High Court case against the builder/developer and other related parties.

So dear reader, I do understand emotional overwhelm, distress and chaos. But I also know first-hand how crucial it is, to not let your emotions get the upper hand. Life is unpredictable, and there will always be times when situations and people will push us to the edge. In this demanding and fast paced life, each of us are vulnerable to emotional overwhelm and we are all guilty of reacting in ways that are unfitting. Nonetheless, the better equipped you are at managing your emotions, the greater your capacity to bounce back and cope with the many demands and stresses that you will encounter along the way.

Indeed, I am far from perfect in my own emotional management, and I am work in progress with each passing day, as my children will attest to! An important point to understand is this: unless you take charge of your daily feelings and reactions, you will remain a slave to your moods, and as a result you will continue to live a difficult and stress induced life, that will slowly deplete your mojo and invariably steal away your happiness and health. I now know, that had I not focused on developing my own emotional management, I would have fared far worse.

Developing emotional resilience has been the key reason that has kept my spark alight, in order to keep me moving forwards and has continued to act as a buffer against life's inevitable obstacles, setbacks and disappointments. Now, you might be thinking resilience is a trait that a person is either born with or without. This is not true. Developing resilience is a learning process that can be learned by anyone.

I like to call it the bounce-back factor; because at the heart of resilience, is a person's ability to bounce back and re-adjust themselves following stressful and negative experiences. It really is very liberating to realise, that once you begin to develop your emotional resilience, you will start to experience a wave of positive change in your life, as you come to understand that no matter what life throws at you, no matter what stress is encountered, you can overcome and adapt to these difficulties.

Of course that's not to say that you won't still feel the frustration, pain and hurt that goes with difficult experiences, the difference will be in your ability to move through these experiences with less of a negative impact on your life.

Testing Your Own Emotional Health

How is your emotional health today? Interestingly, we are not always aware of how frayed around the edges we have become and that can be attributed to the fact that we usually rationalise away typical warning signs or just don't want to admit it. After all, admitting it may seem like you failed, or you might feel you are not sure how to put it right, or that you will have to do something about it, but you have no time.

A quick way to give yourself an emotional health check is by intentionally noticing how you are interacting in situations, and with others. You'll soon know that you are wearing thin emotionally, if you find yourself bursting into tears easily or lashing out at others more frequently because everyone is grating on your nerves. Perhaps you are making mountains out of molehills, or are creating a drama/crisis out of minor incident. Have your patience and tolerance levels hit an all-time low? These indicators alone speak volumes about your emotional wellbeing, and should act as a red flag, to take positive action to restore your emotional health.

Being human equates to us being emotional beings with emotionally driven behaviour. For example when we get stressed, we have a tendency to lash out at others and say hurtful things. We then justify our reaction at the time, but with hindsight, guilt comes knocking on our door. We feel guilty and berate ourselves, which leaves us feeling even more stressed and insecure. Then when we feel out of control and insecure, we turn to others for approval. As a result, we say 'yes' when we really mean 'no' because we want to please, even if it is to our detriment. When we feel inferior, we may resort to gossip or look for fault in others so that we feel better about ourselves, and when we get bored we over indulge or behave excessively. When we worry, we have a tendency to make matters worse by imagining the worst case scenario, leaving us feeling even more fearful. And on and on our emotional self goes sailing close to the edge of burnout.

The fact is that our thoughts and behaviours become so habitual and ingrained into the fibres of our being, that we just go with it without ever questioning ourselves, even if our reactions are detrimental to our wellbeing. As a result we are quick to make judgements, to criticise, to assume or jump to conclusions without ever pausing between our thoughts and actions, leaving us feeling like worn out rejects.

The Mind Gap - If you are a seasoned traveller you will have come across intercom announcements at rail stations that warn you to 'Mind the Gap' - that space between the train and platform. What I have come to learn is that most people's 'mind gap' - that space between their thoughts and actions - is full to the brim.

Congested with thoughts about things that need doing, past regrets, harbouring resentments or worrying about people, events and the 'what if's' of the future. All this noise, swerving and weaving through the mind, means that nothing actually flows.

A congested mind will always interfere with our ability to think clearly and rationally, and that in turn acts as a barrier to emotional wellness. By creating a momentary gap between our thoughts and actions, we effectively interrupt this habitual emotional re-activity, so that we can gain fresh perspective.

I'm sure you can recall many times when you were feeling unhinged, or in a distressed state and done and said things that you wished you had not, but had no idea how to stop it. It just happened - similar to pressing the send button on a mobile text, wishing that you could somehow freeze time and retract the message. We have all been there, I'm sure.

In order to get on with the business of living well, you will need to find a way to 'Pause,' breathe and take a mental step back, in order to bounce back with a renewed kick-ass mindset.

Part II and Part III covers this in great detail, through a set of processes that I call 'System Pause.'

PART II

STOP EMOTIONAL REACTIVITY

Chapter 4

Introducing System Pause

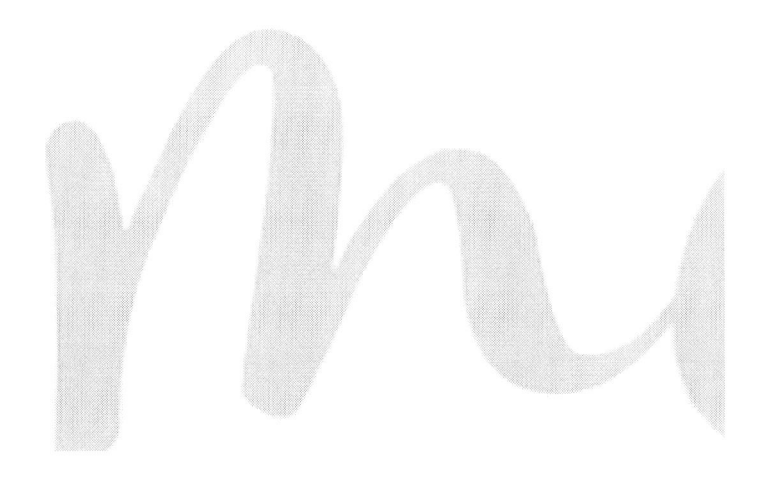

System Pause Explained - A vital part of being able to minimise the impact of stress and negative experiences is through the development of emotional resilience, as mentioned previously. I thought long and hard about the process by which I would guide you on how to do this, which led to much research in this area from a variety of disciplines, science research and books.

What emerged was that people who are resilient often share a combination of core traits that work together synergistically. In other words, these particular characteristics accomplish more when they are utilised together than they could alone. I also wanted to include a tool that could be accessed anytime, anywhere particularly during emotionally fragile times. With so many tools out there for living better, my focus is on guiding you through a system that is practical and easy to remember, which is why I chose to wrap these core characteristics around an acronym called System PAUSE.

Divided into two stages, the first stage 'Pause for Breath' guides you through a breathing technique that effectively operates like a mental braking system. It helps to induce a state of calm during times of emotional overwhelm and anxiety.

Stage two, 'Pause for Resilience' hones in on these five core characteristics, and draws out in great detail, the 'why' and 'how to' of each characteristic, so that you get to understand and learn ways to mitigate the negative impact of stressful events, whilst protecting your emotional and physical wellbeing. Each characteristic builds up sequentially, revealing the power and science behind each – 'Positivity, Acceptance, Undeterred, Self-Care and Empathy.' There are also several activities that you are guided through, to reinforce learning.

P → Positive
A → Acceptance
U → Undeterred
S → Self - Care
E → Empathy

BREATHE

Get Ready To Pause For Breath

Stage one

Pause is an incredibly powerful word, as it simply means to STOP. When we stop 'doing', we usually just breathe, take a mental step back and gain fresh perspective. How often are you swept away in the heat of the moment, or the chaos of a situation, that you forget to just breathe and consider how best to respond at that time? The same can be said about those crazily busy days, where you feel that you have been chasing your tail all day.

By utilizing your breath correctly, you effectively create a mental braking system, which will allow you to not only slow down and gain fresh perspective, but also to regain control during emotionally intense moments. Think about the last time you were worried, stressed or felt wound up. Did you notice how you were breathing? It is likely that unless you were experiencing a panic attack, you were not aware of your breath. Since we are breathing all of the time, we take our breath for granted, which is not surprising given that we take anywhere between 17,000 – 30,000 breaths per day on average – or more.

Most of the time our breathing is done so involuntary, but what many people fail to realise is that our breath is dual controlled. In other words, our breathing happens both consciously and unconsciously, it is not just an involuntary process. Think about it, if you choose so now, you can hold your breath, slow your breath or speed it up. You can draw your breath through your nose or mouth.

The crucial point here is this, you do have control. Yet during stressful or busy times, feeling in control may seem like a distant memory, particularly when others are at the receiving end of your re-active behaviour. You may not realise this, but we are hard wired to react defensively, mother-nature ensured that we came equipped with a survival system, so that should we perceive a threat, our chances of survival are increased.

Think of our ancestors going about their day either trying to fight or run from a woolly mammoth or sabre-toothed tiger. Now that you've got the picture, this system which is inherently a part of our human make-up is more commonly known as the fight/flight, or stress response. It is what our body does as it prepares to confront or avoid danger.

Thankfully, in today's world a physical threat like that of our ancestors is unlikely, however, there are a lot of people who live day to day rushing about the place, often with an all-consuming sense of worry, stress and overwhelm, and whilst there may not be a physical threat present, our nervous system cannot tell the difference between a real physical threat or a psychological one.

Money worries, job stress, relationship difficulties, traffic jams, starting a new job/business, getting married, moving home, etc, can all trigger this survival system. In fact, of the several times I go to my kids sports events, I see many parents and sport coaches get wound up when watching their kids compete in a game. And here is where the problem arises - when this all-natural system is triggered frequently, trouble often comes knocking at your mental and physical doors.

Of the many changes that occur once the stress response is activated, our breath is one of the key changes, shifting from a slow, measured breath to a fast, shallow one. As a result our body is subjected to a host of changes, whilst our immune system is suppressed, thereby exposing us to an increased risk of disease and illness. It is suggested that it can take up to 72 hours before the body returns to normal biochemically[7], which means, if during that time the stress response is activated, you remain in a constant state of stress. This in turn can lead to burn out, resulting in mental decline and depression.

Now think of how many times you got flustered, annoyed, worried and so forth in the last 72 hours. Additionally, we develop poor habits of breathing due to poor posture and a more sedentary lifestyle. As I said earlier in the section on body talk, we have become a nation of slumpers. Crunched up behind the wheel of a car or hunched over a desk for several hours at a time, or just sitting on the couch means that we are not taking full breaths and therefore we are using less of our lung capacity.

A great way to see correct breathing in action is to notice how a baby or a young, relaxed child breathes. You will notice that their belly inflates with each breath in and deflates with each out breath. Little movement will be noticed in the upper chest area. Yet, chest breathing has become the norm for many people all over the world.

Is it then any wonder that many people complain of feeling fatigued and stressed most of the time?

The way we breathe is vital to our health and wellbeing, and if correct breathing is practiced daily, the side effects are profound. Breathing influences our physiology and moods, and by learning to diaphragmatically breathe (belly breathing), you can turn down feelings of anxiety and stress and recalibrate yourself to a calmer state in just a couple of minutes.

Correct breathing techniques have always been fundamental to the ancient practices of meditation and yoga, and articles and websites teaching proper breathing techniques are plentiful on the internet.

In fact it was Herbert Benson, MD, who brought mass market appeal to the idea of diaphragmatic breathing through his first book, 'The Relaxation Response.' Herbert Benson, MD, is a renowned pioneer in Mind, Body Medicine and the collection of his papers are part of the Harvard medical Library Collection.

The mechanics behind this all natural practice is simple, and the only equipment needed is your lungs.

It involves triggering the body's relaxation branch of the brain through controlled breathing. Usually this is done by inhaling slowly through the nose for a few seconds, ensuring that the belly expands, holding the breath for a few seconds and exhaling completely and slowly through the mouth for a count longer than inhaled.

Many suggest a breathing pattern of 4:7:8.

That means inhale on the count of four, hold for the count of seven and exhale for the count of eight. Explore what works for you in terms of length of breath in, hold and out - so long as your breath out is longer than when you inhale.

Let's give it a go.

Practicing Pause For Breath

In the very moment that you notice that you are feeling overwhelmed, or you begin to feel an intense emotional sensation, do the following:

Pause – Drop your shoulders down, close your mouth and take a slow breath through your nose for a mental count of four. Whilst doing this, I like to imagine taking one step back as I inhale and count. This acts as a mental cue to step back from whatever is causing me to feel the negative sensation.

Hold your breath for a mental count of seven. Ensure that your shoulders remain relaxed, and that your posture is upright but soft. In other words, adjust yourself so that you are not hunched forwards or holding your shoulders tensely.

As you exhale, breathe out through your mouth slowly and completely for a mental count of eight. When breathing out through your mouth, purse your lips as if gently blowing out a candle.

This breathing cycle should be repeated for at least four cycles, which is just under one and half minutes. However, in order to feel the immediate relief and benefits that this technique offers, it is recommended that you practice a minimum of four breathing cycles, as outlined above, twice a day, and ideally as often as possible. To maximise oxygen intake and to activate your body's natural relaxation response, it is important to breathe from your belly.

Avoid getting too caught up with the counting aspect initially, so long as you slowly inhale via the belly, pause for a small time, and slowly exhale for a little longer than inhalation.

Testing your current breathing habits:

Sit up straight in a chair, feet uncrossed.

Place one hand on your chest and the other hand across your belly just above your navel.

Breathe as you normally would and see if you can notice which hand rise's more. If you are breathing correctly, your belly hand should rise more than your chest.

Breathing is one the most natural, straightforward and powerful practices that you can do for yourself. It may feel awkward initially as you re-learn to breathe from your abdomen, so be mindful of your inner critic should you find yourself getting irritated or annoyed. With practice, it will begin to feel more natural as you feel more at ease.

Because our lives are filled with a medley of distractions and dramas, we often forget to just breathe. By intentionally changing your breath as described in this section, you will regain an immediate sense of control, which will also bring immediate benefits even if you have not perfected it.

PART III

FIVE BEST WAYS TO BOUNCE BACK

Chapter 5

The Power & Science of Positivity

> **'If you change the way you look at things, the things you look at change'[15]**

'Think Positive' is no doubt something that all of us have had said to us at some point in our life, and I suspect that like me, it rubbed you up the wrong way. Despite it being said with good intentions, when you are feeling less than positive about a situation, it can be difficult to take this comment on board. In fact, being told to think positive can be counter-productive at times, especially if you have tried to no avail.

Other times, you may not just want to think positive, because being negative might offer you some level of comfort or justification about the situation you find yourself in.

It is now widely accepted that having a positive outlook enables us to cope better with life's set-backs and frustrations; this in turn reduces the harmful effects of stress in the body. If that isn't enough to convince you, let me share with you some thought-provoking research that I came across in my endeavours to demonstrate to you, the importance of cultivating a positive attitude within your life.

Dr. Masaru Emoto came into the international spotlight during the 1990's for his water experiments. A researcher and doctor of alternative medicine, Dr. Emoto claimed that molecules of water are affected by our thoughts, words and feelings[8]. To demonstrate his claim, he placed samples of water into a freezer labelled with negative and positive words. Phrases like, 'Thank You' and 'You Fool', in various languages were used.

Once frozen and crystals formed, photographs were taken. Interestingly the samples that had been exposed to the positive words formed beautiful crystals, while samples that had been exposed to more negative phrases, like 'you fool' had either distorted crystals or did not form any crystals.

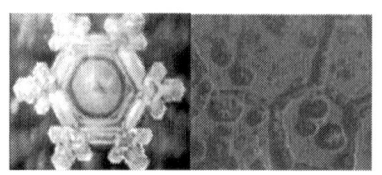

Thank you   You fool

Astounded by his findings, he then began to observe the effects of prayer, music and images on his water samples. Again, his results indicated that water crystal formations were also affected; reinforcing his belief that emotional energies and vibrations could change the physical structure of water. Given this theory and the fact that we human beings are composed of over 60% water, the impact of our own attitudes on our health and wellbeing have the potential to be life transforming.

Dr. Emoto appeared not to value scientific methods which brought his name and work into disrepute by the scientific community. However, I draw a very simple conclusion. There are innumerable companies today that profit from selling products that offer quick-fix solutions for achieving wellness and good health. You don't have to be lured by the temptations of these quick-fix promises.

Whatever conclusions you draw from Dr. Emoto's experiments, one thing is clear. A positive attitude creates a happier biochemistry, resulting in a healthier mind and body.

With or without the demonstrations of his work, it is widely accepted, and well documented that there is a direct connection between how we think and how we feel, and that our immune system is linked with our emotions.

Whilst negative events are an inevitable part of our lives, a negative attitude is not.

Shifting Perspective

Your experience of life is essentially shaped by the perspective you view it from. Being more positive or negative can create two different realities. Some people can take painful and negative situations and find a way to shift their focus on the positive aspects, leaving them feeling empowered and strong, whilst others remain stuck in the negativity pit to the point where they can develop what I call a martyr mind.

Many of us if not all of us slip into a martyr mentality from time to time, but when you set up camp there, you begin to function in a victim level of awareness, frequently talking about how tough things are, choosing to stay in the misery rather than find a way out of it.

'It is easy to be positive when things are going your way', I often hear people say. But that isn't necessarily true. I have observed people who have achieved many of their dream goals, yet their daily life experience is a struggle, filled with stress and drama. On the other hand, I know of people for whom life has truly tested them with very difficult, painful or traumatic experiences, yet they show up each day putting their best foot forward, grateful for their blessings.

Don't misunderstand me, being more positive does not mean not having off days, where finding the positive in a situation is not always possible. Nor does it mean sticking your head in the sand in the hope of avoiding painful emotions. Embracing a positive mindset is more about developing smarter thinking that is self-supporting and based on rational thought.

Interestingly, we all have a tendency to pick up irrational ways of thinking along the way that fly under the radar of our awareness. In fact, whilst writing this book, cultivating a positive attitude became my greatest challenge to date.

In early 2015, the dark claws of dementia took hold of my Dad's mind and stole him away from his family. I had never known pain like it - to witness the rapid demise of a gentleman, who was high spirited and had a zest for life.

Renowned for his dapper looks and his powerful musical renditions of Frankie Lane's 'Mule Train', 'Ghost Riders in the Sky' and Jonny Cash's 'Burning Ring of Fire', this proud and energetic man, my Dad, had his life, as he had known it, snatched from him as he battled his way within the abyss of this cruel and horrid disease.

As I was half way through writing this book, my Dad passed away. There are no ways to reframe this experience in order to find the positive, for there is none. Instead, I shift my focus away from dwelling on the loss, hurt and anger, the 'why's', and the 'how's'. I now purposely call to my mind the many positives for having my life blessed by such a wonderful Dad.

Putting your Life into Perspective

Here's my point, there is a way of being, your emotional default setting if you like, which can be developed. Regardless of your past experiences or your current circumstances, you can change the way you look at things, and by doing so, you can change the way you feel and act. I realise, that some of you may think that this is an oversimplification, however, Cognitive Behavioural Therapy stems from this premise.

How often do you wish you did not feel a certain way, but believe that it is outside of your control?

Isn't it true, that when we get mad, sad, upset, etc, we believe it to be as a result of others or some external situation? This is further reinforced in the way we speak: "She made me so mad", or "He ruined my day" etc. The truth of the matter is that it is usually our interpretation of an event that triggers our emotional reactions. In other words, how we explain things to ourselves, also known as our self-talk. This is precisely why you have a group of people who experience the same event or situation, yet have different emotional responses.

Let's use sky diving (the external situation) as an example. A group of holiday makers all eager to try sky diving - three of the five revel in the fun and thrill of the experience, whilst the other two experience dread and panic. Yet the situation was identical for them all.

A few years ago, I remember watching 'I'm a Celebrity Get me Out of Here' and the contestants were challenged with jumping from an airplane into the jungle. Each celebrity, all bar one, jumped, stressed to the gills, with their eyes shut screaming with fear and dread as they descended. Just one celebrity exclaimed: "Wow, what a lucky girl I am, to have this wonderful opportunity," as she soaked up the beauty and splendour of all that was around her, in the beauty of the Australian rainforest, whilst falling down to earth. She was Stacey Solomon, who went on to win the show, and I believe that it was her positive mental attitude that had made that possible.

Here are another couple of examples, of how easily we get pulled into the grip of negative feelings.

A woman driving through a tunnel begins to feel her heart pound, mouth go dry and she starts to feel anxious and sweaty. The tunnel is busy with traffic and her car comes to a halt. The heavy hand of dread weighs down on her chest as thoughts of death loom.

A man driving along the road becomes agitated when another driver begins to tailgate him. In his agitated state he starts to slow down to teach this road offender a lesson. Agitation soon escalates to infuriation when the tailgater swerves past and cuts across him. As he pumps hard on the horn, screaming a string of profanities, the man is left feeling angry and stressed, and arrives at his destination feeling out of sorts, repeating his woeful tale to anyone willing to listen. Meanwhile the tailgater has moved on with his life.

The above scenarios are all too familiar for many people, and it is situations like this that are very real for several people, whom I might add, think that these situations are beyond their control.

Looking at the woman driving in the tunnel, the physiological sensations of the heart pounding, tight chest, breathlessness and dry mouth were triggered by thoughts that were not obvious to the woman at the time.

On closer examination, it becomes clear that on entering the tunnel, this woman begun to think that someone had crashed as the traffic was heavier than normal. She thought, "If someone crashed, I could be trapped here for hours." Her chest began to tighten. "What if there is not enough air to breath, especially with all this traffic and the fumes, how would I cope?" "What if a fire breaks out, oh God the tunnel is built under water - I won't be able to hold my breath or swim." The more catastrophic her thinking, the intensity of her emotions heightened, causing her to think that she may pass out, or worse still, have a heart attack because of the sensations in her chest.

In the second scenario, the man feels justified in slowing down to teach the tailgater a lesson. His attitude was "Who does this person think they are, putting my life and others lives at danger." "He should know better, he should not be allowed on the road or have a license at this rate." "I'll teach him a lesson."

By slowing down, his actions made this situation worse, causing the other driver to overtake him, placing him at more risk as he does so. The more he thought how he 'should' not be on the road, how he 'should' not put him in that predicament, the more stressed he became.

Can you understand how it was their attitudes that drove each of their emotional reaction?

Don't misunderstand me, there are several times when I get hot under the collar or get my nose put out of joint, and I enjoy a good rant. My children will testify to that! However if you're attitude is increasingly causing a disturbance to the quality of your life, then it may be a red flag to do something about it.

Changing your attitude does not mean going from feeling really angry to happy, it means changing your perspective so that you feel less angry. If you feel very anxious, it is adjusting you're attitude so that you feel less anxious. If you feel miserable, it is adjusting you're attitude so that you feel less miserable and so on.

In order to cultivate a more positive attitude, you will need to clear the way to begin with and that will mean being very honest with yourself. How are your moods dominating your life? In what way are they causing a disturbance to you and others? If you decided today to go for it, to de-weed all that overgrown negativity and fully immerse yourself into feeling positive about some aspects of your life, what would you need to think, say and do differently?

Why not try it now. Get out a notepad and pen and start making notes.

Here are some ideas to help get you started. You may find doing this a little difficult as we all have blind spots. Blind spots, in this instance, are certain fixed ways of thinking, in other words, our beliefs that we develop over time and become our norm, even if they are self defeating. Here are some examples:-

Uncover Your Blind Spots

Doomsday Thinking - Do you frequently jump to the worse possible scenario? I call this doomsday thinking, more commonly called catastrophic thinking, which is portrayed very well in this quote by a respected philosopher of the French Renaissance, Michel De Montaigne:-

"My life is full of terrible misfortunes, most of which never happened."

Many people overestimate the likelihood of negative things happening, much like the example of the women driving through the tunnel. A sensation in the chest turns out to be an impending heart-attack, the fun of a family holiday, is superseded by thoughts of a plane crash on the return journey.

I recall a colleague calling me in a distressed state, because she received an unexpected call from her boyfriend asking if she would come by his home after work. She spent that afternoon wondering why he wanted her to drop by, and had convinced herself that he was ending the relationship with her. It turns out that he had planned a surprise for her.

Continuing to think something bad will happen, will invariably lead to a life filled with fear and anxiety, leaving no room for positivity to flourish.

Shoulds - How often do you 'should' your way through the day? If you're anything like me, should is up there on the top ten of your vocabulary list. After all, when used correctly it can be a useful moral too.

Unfortunately most people seem to use 'should' in the context that leaves them and others feeling undermined. "She should have been more considerate of my feelings," "I should not have eaten that desert," "He should have asked me my opinion first," "She should have apologised," "I should have spoken up for myself," and on and on we go 'shoulding' at others and at ourselves, provoking feelings of frustration, anger, disappointments and resentments.

Whilst we all feel strongly about what should be done and said in certain situations, these ideas about how someone 'should' or 'should not' behave are pointless. Fuelled by pressure, expectations and judgements, the only thing that 'should' does, is that it gets you upset!

> 'If you continuously compete with others, you become bitter: if you continuously compete with yourself you become better.'[9]

Compare and Despair - In this age of social media, we have constant access to the personal lives of others. Whether it's close friends, family, colleagues or celebrities, we are privy to their latest holidays, weekend retreats, newest purchases, their achievements, their latest romance and other such intimate details. Looking at other's lives from the outside can get us wondering about our own inadequacies and shortfalls, resulting in an over focus on the negative aspects of our own life, rather than counting our blessings.

Do you recall at the introduction of this book, when I said "many people looking from the outside in thought I had it all - the champagne lifestyle, the stable relationship, plush apartment overlooking the beach, luxury car, exotic holidays, yet surrounded by all this glitz and glamour, I never felt more alone."

Comparisons are foolish because we usually base them on assumptions we make about another. In this lifetime, there will always be people greater and lesser than us, and there will always be more to want. The only measuring stick that you can truly measure yourself against, is the person you were yesterday.

To continue to compare yourself to others will keep you on the negativity rollercoaster and steal you of happiness and peace of mind. These are only some of the many self-defeating thoughts that we pick up along our journey. Once you acknowledge that your emotional responses are linked with your thinking, you will be able to train yourself to view situations from other perspectives and develop a more self-supporting style of thinking and positive attitude.

Learning how is simply a matter of utilizing PAUSE - using your breath as practiced earlier, turn your attention inward and notice the thoughts that ran through your mind prior to feeling an negative emotion.

Once you begin to make efforts to consciously notice your thoughts that are leading to negative emotional states, you can then go about changing them. The goal is to eliminate irrational or fixed thinking, and replace them with more rational and self-supporting thoughts that in turn paves the way for a happier and more resilient you.

You may not always get it right, but the key is to know that you need to start looking for those thoughts at the time. That way, you are in control and no longer hand over power to your moods.

The fact is that life feels so much better with a positive attitude therefore it makes good sense to protect it at all costs.

Gratitude

Other ways to stimulate a positive attitude include expressing gratitude. Whilst I was researching the science behind gratitude, I came across many studies that all have one thing in common. Counting your blessings rather than your misfortunes contributed significantly to a happier and healthier wellbeing. I myself have seen great results whilst coaching people that feel overcome by negativity within their lives.

These people were given the task of creating a 'gratitude journal' and were asked to write in a special notebook each evening, at least five good and positive things that they would have experienced that day in which they were grateful for. They were also asked to bring a smile to their face as they recalled those things.

Despite finding it difficult initially, once they persevered, they noticed that their general attitude to life had changed for the better.

All too often I hear people complain that they are not appreciated at work or by their spouse. And the irony is that they are equally guilty of the very thing they accuse their partner or employer of – not being grateful or appreciative of what they do have, and it is only when they have lost their job, for example, that they realise how lucky they really were. I have come to understand particularly these past few years that cultivating gratitude is a choice.

For example, you may well feel under-appreciated at work or at home, but you can always acknowledge all the positives that being employed or sharing your life with loved ones bring to your life, instead of feeling under-valued.

I have to say feeling hard done by these past several years could have easily been a justified and dominant feeling for me and my family. Especially as we still await for justice around the debacle of our family home and all the consequences that spin out of that.

But gratitude is a deliberate practice of appreciating what we do have, instead of focusing on what is lacking. Often we only realise our blessings when they are no longer there. We take for granted what we already have, including our health and people that bless our lives until the day they're gone or we are sat in the waiting room of a doctor's surgery recounting thoughts of 'if only' or 'what if.'

If you are like me a mum of two children with bedrooms strewn with clothes, muddy boots and other often indescribable apparel that is evident of young lives as they grow, be aware that all this will disappear all too soon and we will find ourselves wishing for a time machine to take us back to those chaotic times. An unclean house will no longer seem important.

Yes, it is an injustice that several years on, I am still waiting to have our day in court to seek a fair resolution for my family home. Yes, it is deeply saddening to live in an age where there is gross breakdown in a public health system that could not look after my Dad's needs in the way he deserved. Yes, I am tired from unrelenting calls and letters from a bank that endeavours to repossess a home that is structurally beyond living in. However, rather than brooding over these misfortunes, (and the lure of brooding is often quite strong), I choose to remain thankful for what I do have and acknowledge this daily.

I smile as my mum, who is now not too far off 80, inspires me in so many ways. She often calls me by phone several times daily, usually not at the most convenient of times. I can view it as an interruption to my day or I can acknowledge it as a pause from 'doing' so that I can 'be' with her. To connect with her, to listen to her, to give her my time, for I know the sense of loss and loneliness she feels without my Dad is deafening.

I have no doubt that her days must often feel like weeks especially during the dark winter months. I am grateful to both my parents for giving me life, for what they have sacrificed in order to provide for their children – all seven of us!

With so many things competing for our time, it can be easy to overlook those that might need it the most. There are so many ways that we can practice gratitude and giving my time is one way that I honour this practice.

I hear people say daily: "I haven't got time, or I wish I had more time to do xyz."

Time is an interesting concept; and I often find myself asking if it really is time that we lack. It's as if we have become prisoners of the clock, rushing about the place in an endless flurry of doing, blinded by problem-focused thinking. We convince ourselves we haven't got time, and then look over our shoulder with regret when we lose something or someone that we cherished or valued.

Whatever time you think you lack, pause and make the time to smell the scent of love, friendship and life that surrounds you and give thanks.

The following story is an excellent example of how we can all get blinded by life's hassles that we often forget to look around us.

The Black Dot

'One day a professor entered the classroom and asked his students to prepare for a surprise test. They waited anxiously at their desks for the test to begin. The professor handed out the question paper, with the text facing down as usual. Once he handed them all out, he asked his students to turn the page and begin. To everyone's surprise, there were no questions, just a black dot in the centre of the page.

The professor, seeing the expression on everyone's face, told them "I want you to write what you see there." The confused students; got started on the inexplicable task.

At the end of the class, the professor took all the answer papers and started reading every one of them aloud in front of all the students. All of them, with no exceptions described the black dot, trying to explain its position in the middle of the sheet, etc.

After each one had been read, the classroom stayed silent as the professor began to explain: "I am not going to grade you on this - I just wanted to give you something to think about. No one wrote about the white part of the paper. Everyone focused on the black dot – and the same happens in our lives. We have a white paper to observe and enjoy, but we always focus on the dark spots. Our life is a gift given to us by God, with love and care, and we always have reasons to celebrate – nature renewing itself every day, our friends around us, the job that provides our livelihood, the miracles we see every day. However, we insist on focusing only on the dark spots – the health issues that bother us, the lack of money, the complicated relationship with a family member, the disappointment with a friend, etc. The dark spots are very small compared to everything we have in our lives, but they are the ones that pollute our minds."

The Lesson – "Take your eyes away from the black spots in your life. Enjoy each one of your blessings, each moment that life gives you."

I realise that we all get pulled in the direction of only noticing all that is wrong or that which we lack; after all we are bombarded daily with adverts and messages about how much better we would feel if we had more. However, as you begin this daily practice of expressing gratitude, you will be surprised as to how your perception of your life changes for the better. From today, you can foster an attitude of gratitude and positivity that induces a feeling of empowerment and excitement about life, or one that fosters negativity that creates a feeling of helplessness and a crisis-driven mentality.

Of course, it does not happen overnight, but moving towards a more optimistic way of being yields high rewards. With time and practice, this mental state of positivity will grow stronger.

Exercise – An Attitude of Gratitude Journal

Five things I am grateful for today

1.

2.

3.

4.

5.

Chapter 6

Acceptance
Finding Inner Peace

> **'When we live our lives fighting against our circumstances we move into an unresourceful state**[10]**'**

'An elderly Chinese woman had two large pots, each hung on the ends of a pole, which she carried across her neck. One of the pots had a crack in it, while the other pot was perfect and always delivered a full portion of water. At the end of the long walk from the stream to the house, the cracked pot arrived only half full. This went on daily for two years, with the woman bringing home only one and a half pots of water. Of course, the perfect pot was proud of its accomplishments.

But the poor cracked pot was ashamed of its own imperfection, and miserable that it could only do half of what it had been made to do. After two years of what it perceived to be bitter failure, it spoke to the woman one day by the stream: "I am ashamed of myself, because this crack in my side causes water to leak out all the way back to your house."

The old woman smiled, "Did you notice that there are flowers on your side of the path, but not on the other pot's side? That's because I have always known about your flaw, so I planted flower seeds on your side of the path, and every day while we walk back, you water them. For two years, I have been able to pick these beautiful flowers, to decorate the table. Without you being just the way you are, there would not be this beauty to grace the house."

At the core of this heart warming story is acceptance; acceptance of life circumstances, acceptance of our complete self and that of others. Each and every one of us has our own unique flaws, idiosyncrasies and imperfections that make our lives more colourful and enriching. However, when we live our lives fighting against our circumstances, rejecting ourselves and judging others, we put ourselves into an un-resourceful state, where stress and struggle become all too familiar companions.

You may not like aspects of yourself, you may wish that things turned out differently, you may continue to wish that certain circumstances hadn't happened, and you might wish you had a different house, partner, better family, job etc. To continue trying to change your circumstances by wishing they never happened, is like wishing that time would stand still.

The tide of time comes and goes regardless of anyone or anything, as does the many circumstances of your life. All the wishing and arguing cannot change things in that moment. Yet, many of us try to live our lives caught up in an emotional tug of war, hopelessly pulling and pushing against our current reality. I realise that it's particularly hard to practice acceptance when you deeply wish things aren't the way they are.

To be honest in 2002, when I relocated back home to Ireland with my suitcase of dreams ready to be unpacked, I never envisaged there would be so many hardships and pitfalls. But when things happen, which invariably they do, and not always in the way you had hoped or dreamed for, rather than creating additional pain, stress and misery for yourself by arguing with why it should not have happened, why it's not fair; bringing some level of acceptance is by far, a more empowering and effective way in bringing about inner peace and change.

'It is what it is' is a universal saying, which I believe instils a sense of acceptance in a situation. Some may see it as helplessness but I see it differently. To me, it's about facing your circumstances as they are, without the inner struggle of over thinking things and wishing things were different.

Simply put, it is about meeting reality at where it is and letting go of the emotional struggle that so often perpetuates the stress and torment of a situation.

What I have learned with my ongoing practice of acceptance is this. Being more accepting is not about disregarding or ignoring our circumstances, nor is it about condoning the actions or behaviour of others. It is also not about not feeling. "I am fine, I'll get over it," is not an indication of emotional resilience.

Of course I was infuriated by the many difficulties I experienced during those challenging years, and indeed I still feel angry, frustrated and flabbergasted by the unfathomable delays in bringing a resolution to this crazy situation involving my family home.

I still struggle to understand why these people whom were involved in the build of our broken home continue to play a game with our lives. Is it not enough that they have already denied me, my children and husband of a sense of security and stability these past eight years? I am bewildered by the legal system, and the length of time it is taking to bring, what is a clear cut situation to a resolution.

I am also disgusted by the arrogant and unscrupulous stance the bank has taken, despite my several attempts to negotiate a resolution. So you see, I still feel the pain that accompanies this very difficult situation. But rather than dwell on this, which will invariably keep me stuck in feelings of anger, resentment and disappointment, I choose to take responsibility for my personal happiness, and that is where I believe acceptance stems from.

No matter how justified I feel for pointing the finger at these selfish and irresponsible individuals, it is me alone that is responsible for my own future happiness.

It would be foolish of me to allow my mental well being to hinge on the actions of these people.

So, if you are someone who is currently facing a challenge and change, or who tends to feel exacerbated when things turn out differently or don't go according to plan, remember it is you who are ultimately responsible for your future and happiness. We are not always able to control what happens to us, but we can control how we respond to what happens. Pointing the finger of blame, no matter how justified, will ultimately disable you in creating a better future for yourself.

There is a great freedom in spending your energy in building the new rather than on fighting the old. Today, start with where you are now, not with where you should, could or would have been if someone or something did or did not happen. All you ever really have is now, and the outcome of tomorrow will stem from what you do as of now.

On the other hand if accepting yourself is an issue, and you are highly self-critical, struggling with aspects of yourself, whether that's body image or personality characteristics, the following extract may help you to anchor your thoughts in a more rational way.

It was written by the renowned therapist and author, Virgina Satir, in response to a question given to her by an angry teenage girl. Satir was an inspirational lady of her day, and regarded by many people, as the mother of family therapy, due to her pioneering work.

I Am Me

In the whole world, there is not one exactly like me. Everything that comes out of me is authentically mine because I choose it. I own everything about me, my body, my feelings, my mouth, my voice, all my actions, whether they be to others or to myself.

I own my fantasies, my dreams, my hopes, my fears. I own all of my triumphs and successes, all of my failures and mistakes and because I own all of me, I can become intimately acquainted with me and by so doing, I can love me and be friendly with me in all my parts.

I know there are aspects about myself that puzzle me and other aspects I do not know, but as long as I am friendly and loving to myself, I can courageously look for solutions to the puzzles and for ways to find out more about me. However I look and sound, whatever I say and do and whatever I think and feel, at a given moment in time, is authentically me.

If, later some parts of how I looked, sounded, thought and felt turned out to be unfitting, I can discard that which is unfitting and keep the rest, and invest in something new toward my personal growth. I can see, hear, feel, think, say and do.

I have the tools to survive, to be close to others, to be productive, and to make sense and order out of the world of people and things outside of me.

I own me, and therefore I can engineer me and I AM OKAY.

'I own me, therefore I can engineer me'- there is so much power in that statement, don't you think? Once you accept the truth of that, there is infinite possibility for you.

I AM are two of the most powerful words in the dictionary - what you choose to follow with - can tear you down or lift you up. Depending on the label you stamp on yourself, it can render you useful or useless, lovable or unlovable, powerful or powerless and so on. When we utter negative, "I am" phrases to ourselves regularly, they become a part of how we relate to ourselves and we begin to dislike who we are.

Instead, know that you are not your faults or shortcomings. You may engage in stupid behaviour, but that doesn't make you a stupid person always. You might have a bad game, but that does not equate to you been bad at the game. You might fail in certain situations but that does not make you a failure as a person.

Once you bring a level of acceptance to your life and detach yourself from the negative labels, you can switch from a mindset to that of possible instead of impossible. "I am useless, I can't get a job," becomes "I find it difficult to find employment right now, or I find it difficult doing interviews." Do you see that once you detach yourself from the label of "I am useless", you automatically put yourself into a more resourceful state?

Understand that it is easier to change behaviour, than to change an identity; and you really are much more than your behaviours. The key to this is to remember that behaviours are habits, and habits can always be changed.

Also worth doing, is to allow yourself to make mistakes without criticism. Throw away the beat me up stick once and for all and give yourself the space to make mistakes. And when you do get frustrated or disgruntled, bring your sense of humour to the fore.

So you made a mistake, took a step back, so what?

So long as the wheels of progress are turning in the general direction of your goal, you will get there.

As Tony Robbins puts it – "No matter how many mistakes you make or how slow you progress, you're still way ahead of everyone who isn't trying"

The magic of Old Wisdom

I also like the Serenity Prayer, as I believe it captures the true essence and morale of acceptance. Circ 1930's and authored by an American theologian, Reinhold Niebhur, the message is simple, yet truly profound.

"God, grant me the serenity to accept the things I can't change, the courage, to change the things I can, and the wisdom to know the difference."

Exercise

Positive Reframing

List as many negative "I Am" statements that you can bring to mind and try to reframe them into positive statements

- I am
  ....
- I am
  ....
- I am
  ....
- I am
  ....
- I am
  ....

Chapter 7

Developing A 'Can Do' Attitude

Winning at Life

> 'A river cuts through a rock not because of its power but its persistence.'[11]

Being undeterred simply means persevering despite obstacles and setbacks. Although I don't hear the word used often, presumably because the word perseverance is more commonly used, I love this word. For me, being undeterred is not just about perseverance, it goes over and above that.

The word itself personifies courage, resourcefulness, determination and that 'can do' spirit that is pivotal in relation to the development of emotional resilience.

And you know the exciting thing about this skill; you're already well practiced in this quality. Think about it for a moment. What do you think has brought you from where you are now to where you once were? How many difficulties, set-backs and mistakes have you overcome?

An innumerable amount no less. Perhaps you can also call to mind some goals and achievements you have attained over the course of time. Understand this, you have come this far already as a result of your determination, your courage and your perseverance.

Once you acknowledge this, give yourself a hug and appreciate that unshakeable part of you that has moved you through life's mine fields to date.

Now might also be a good time to go back to your Personal Strengths Inventory, (Chapter 2 p36) and add to that list!

Most of us if not all of us will have read about or known of someone who, despite unrelenting circumstances, forged ahead against all odds. History itself is peppered with such stories that serve to remind us that deep within us all is a reservoir of unwavering strength that we can tap into even when pushed to the limits.

British mountaineer, Joe Simpson is one such example, whose extraordinary tale of survival in the Andes was detailed in a book and movie, 'Touching the Void.' His simple but profound philosophy: "Don't whine, just deal with it," is inspired by a Tibetan phrase; "Ge Garne," which roughly translates to "shit happens."

I have no doubt that this attitude of "When life gives you lemons, make lemonade,"[16] has played a large part in his recovery and ability to walk again, despite him being told that he would not walk again.

Another example is much closer to home and is that of a young lady, Joanne O Riordan, from my hometown of Cork, Ireland. Born with a condition that left her completely without limbs, this resilient young lady had her life story captured in a documentary called 'No limbs, No Limits,' which was screened nationally and inspired the nation. She has addressed the United Nations, publically challenged the Irish Government on cuts to disability and was awarded a scholarship by University College Cork. She has also won the prestigious international 'Outstanding Young Person of the World' award. She lives independently and studied Criminology at College. She once wrote: "I have reached my goals and dreams with various hiccups, but I have never allowed them to hold me back."

So dear reader, you are extraordinary and you have come far. The fact that you live and breathe today confirms this.

You may have grown weary and tired, drained from what might seem like one too many setbacks. But in emotionally turbulent times, when doubts and fears creep in, it is essential to have something that will anchor you during life's stormy seas - that will inspire within you, the resolve to keep on going.

Affirmations

I use affirmations frequently as my anchor. These affirmations are simple statements that I affirm often, especially when the going gets tough, and when I need a jolt in remaining focused and steadfast.

Interestingly the word 'affirm' stems from the Latin word 'affirmare', which as it turns out, means to make steady and to strengthen. And trust me the following affirmations have truly given me strength when I needed it the most.

Rise Each Time You Fall - I truly believe that one of the greatest success principals is not to give up on your goals, and this affirmation always reminds me of a poem that my 11 year-old son shared with me one day, as he witnessed my disbelief in losing a day's work of writing, because I had forgotten to press the save key on my computer.

To me the following poem truly captures the essence of real success in life.

The Race – (abridged) Attribute to Dr. 'Dee' Groberg

Their parents watched from off the side, each cheering for their son, and each boy hoped to show his folks that he would be the one. The whistle blew and off they flew, like chariots of fire, to win, to be the hero there, was each young boy's desire. One boy in particular, whose dad was in the crowd, was running in the lead and thought: "My dad will be so proud." But as he speeded down the field and crossed a shallow dip, the little boy who thought he'd win, lost his step and slipped. As he fell, his hope fell too; he couldn't win it now. Humiliated, he just wished to disappear somehow.

But as he fell his dad stood up and showed his anxious face, which to the boy so clearly said, "Get up and win that race!" So he jumped up to try again, ten yards behind the last. "If I'm to gain those yards," he thought, "I've got to run real fast!" Exceeding everything he had, he regained eight, then ten... but trying hard to catch the lead, he slipped and fell again. "There's no sense running anymore, I'm out! Why try?

But then he thought about his dad, who soon he'd have to face. "Get up," an echo sounded low, "You haven't lost at all." "You were not meant for failure here, get up and win that race." So, up he rose to run once more, refusing to forfeit, and he resolved that win or lose, at least he wouldn't quit. So far behind the others now, the most he'd ever been, still he gave it all he had and ran like he could win. And to his dad he sadly said, "I didn't do so well."

"To me, you won," his father said. "You rose each time you fell."

I'm sure like me you will have found this a heart warming poem as it serves to remind us all that to win in life is no more than just this; to rise each time you fall.

The choice of quitting or going on can be a defining moment in your life. Richard Nixon was noted for saying, "A man is not finished when he is defeated. He is finished when he quits."

Just like the boy in the poem, your success is measured by your willingness to try. So if you are not living your best life now, then your best self is yet to come, and the only way to discover your best, is when you get back up when you are down.

Where you focus your attention will be pivotal, because what you focus on will create energy and momentum. When things don't go according to plan as so often happens, instead of focusing on all that is going wrong, concentrate on why you're doing what you're doing in the first place. And the best way to do that is to define your goals. One of the most effective ways to carry on, in spite of tough times, is to have something to aim for. I discuss goal setting in greater depth, through a step by step process that I call, 'Whole Brain Goal Setting' at the end of this chapter.

Become Part of the Solution Not The Problem - I love this one, as it is an excellent affirmation that serves to remind us all that if we turn our attention towards finding a solution, problems lose their force and fade into the background. Very often when we feel worn out and deflated we become more problem-focused.

The difficulty with problem-focused attention is that it not only decreases motivation and strengthens any negativity that you may be feeling at the time, but it also paralyses you from taking positive action. When you take no action, you then become part of the problem. I have found that by affirming this statement frequently, it can act as a powerful reminder of how resourceful you truly are, if you give yourself half the chance. With a solution-driven mindset energy flows, as you begin to engage in the process of change rather than resist it.

Progress, not Perfection - What I have come to learn is that many of us trip ourselves up with the notion of perfection. How often have you not done something, or thrown the towel in because of, "if I can't give 100%, I might as well not do it' mindset?"

In fact, this became a very important affirmation for me whilst writing this book. When Dad had passed away, I began to procrastinate around writing. I tried to convince myself that I had bitten off more than I could chew. That the timing wasn't right as my mood had hit an all time low and that I would not be able to give it my best.

Because I was feeling low, I had slipped into the 'all or nothing' line of thinking. You may recall when I spoke about blind spots earlier, (Chapter 5, page 82) - you know fixed ways of thinking that are self defeating. Well 'perfectionism' behaviour is intertwined with 'all or nothing thinking' and as a result problems with procrastination will often arise.

If you have gotten yourself into the "I will start 'when' mindset," know that you are on a slippery slope. Waiting until the next day, or "I'll start next week", or until you are the perfect weight, more experienced, more prepared, fitter, better, happier, etc, will set you up for failure because expecting perfection will become overwhelming.

Consequently any efforts to attain your goals will be hindered, which will only serve to deflate your sense of self-worth and in turn increase your vulnerability to stress, anxiety and negativity.

Progress is much more about mini milestones, for which there are a countless number during our lifetime. My best days are usually when I feel I have made some progress, regardless of how small.

Everyday progress, even small accomplishments can make all the difference to our moods; it's a self reinforcing process. The power of small achievements can serve as a catalyst to keep on going through those dark days of doubt and an ebbing motivation.

So the next time you find yourself procrastinating, feel like throwing in the towel or feel overwhelmed by the gravity of your goal, remember the 'Power of Progress' for it is fundamental to your success, and ultimately, your wellbeing.

'Success happens daily, it is not a one-off event. Rather it is the culmination of consistent small steps done over time.'[12]

THE MASTER LIFE SKILL

Whole Brain Goal Setting

Without a shadow of doubt, goal setting gives you focus, direction and ultimately the momentum to carry on. Yet bizarrely of all the skills we learn throughout our schooling, goal setting is on the bottom of the list and that's if it makes it there at all. Nor does it seem to get passed down by our parents as part of our life skills education.

I believe that being goal focused is the key that will unlock that 'I can do spirit' when you feel overwhelmed or defeated. History is steeped with stories of ordinary men and women who have succeeded often defying the odds as a result of their goal focused mind-set. If you are unclear of what exactly a goal is, I will explain.

Goals are conscious decisions about your future; they represent all that you are committed to achieving for yourself and for your life. Of course, the type and quality of your goal will be important in driving your motivation, to keep putting one foot in front of the other, day after day. Sometimes people confuse goals with wishes as they talk about how their life or self will be different someday.

Let me tell you that what you wish for and what you plan for are two very different things. As soon as you set yourself a goal, you effectively set in motion a plan that will give you direction and purpose within your life.

Is there a secret to goal setting?

Secret, no, there is no secret, but there is a technique. Surprisingly it is the subconscious part of our mind that controls much of our behaviour, yet when we set about creating goals or want to change habitual behaviours we rarely if ever connect in with our subconscious. So for example, a person wanting to quit smoking as a goal, consciously decides that they will do so because smoking is bad for their health, costs too much money, is unattractive and is seen these days as anti-social, yet despite all these compelling reasons they fail in their endeavours - why?

This is because no matter how carefully we plan, if there is a mismatch between our conscious minds and subconscious, the subconscious will always win. Our subconscious isn't guided by our conscious instruction; its language is sensory, therefore it is guided by our senses, essentially our imagination.

Let's take the smoker trying to quit example again and another example of somebody trying to lose weight. Day after day the smoker who tries to quit, begins to think about cigarettes, imagining the taste and smell despite their logic for quitting and the person whose goal it is to lose weight may have very clear reasons for dropping weight, but with each passing day this person begins to dwell on how much they miss their favourite food to the point where they can smell or almost taste it. We've all been there. At least I know I have and on more than one occasion.

Both fail in achieving their goal.

In both of these examples, these people spent a great deal of their time imagining the complete opposite of what they were trying to achieve. And then they wonder why they fail.

Note to self, whenever willpower and imagination are in conflict, imagination usually wins.

Never underestimate the power of your imagination. When you incorporate visualizing your goals, what you are effectively doing is activating whole brain activity by tapping into a combination of logic and imagination.

I like to call this process 'Whole Brain Goal Setting.' Although we have one mind, it is important to understand that it can be divided into two functional parts, conscious and subconscious, and it is the subconscious that we need to give extra attention to if we are to be successful in implementing long lasting change within our lives.

By incorporating visualization into your goal setting process, you are invariably connecting your consciously chosen goals to your subconscious mind, thus bringing harmony to both sides so that you're subconscious begins to pursue your goals automatically. In simpler terms, visualizing supports you in your efforts to reach your goals. And a good indicator that you are visualising correctly is when the visualization becomes so real within your mind that you can almost touch or and taste it!

At this point it is also worth highlighting, that of equal importance is your belief that you can achieve whatever goal you plan to pursue. Remember everything appears impossible until the first person does it. A good example of that theory is the four minute mile as described below.

Roger Bannister was knighted for sporting excellence and achieved a goal that was seen as impossible at the time; to run a mile in less than four minutes. It was reported that he refused to subscribe to popular belief that it was impossible to run such a distance within that timeline, and so he set out imagining himself achieving this so called impossible goal.

It is reported that he equally had an unshakeable belief and unwavering commitment to achieve what he believed he had the capacity and inner resources to do. Shortly after his amazing feat, many more athletes went on to smash his record, as early as 46 days later, because a shift in beliefs very quickly took place amongst the sporting community.

Whilst we are all not aspiring record breaking athletes, the point is this. If you are serious about achieving change, then it is of great importance also, that your goals reflect what you believe is possible for you and your ability.

The internet is awash with various goal-setting techniques, should you wish to do some more reading up on goal-setting systems. However, I have outlined below what I believe to be best practice in 'Whole Brain Goal Setting.'

The ABC Approach

Assess your goal.

Believe in your capacity to achieve your goal.

Create your goal.

Assess the goal that you desire - Too often I see people who set out to achieve a personal goal only to have a change of heart half way through, or they give up as soon as they begin. And whilst there may be a number of reasons for this, what I usually find is a lack of mental preparation from the onset.

We all have dreams, hopes and ideas that we can bring to mind, but in order to stay focused and motivated to accomplish these, all goals should really be set on information that you considered at the initial stage, prior to devising your plan of action. Consider carefully the following points before setting your goal out in writing.

Goal Setting Checklist

Consider why you are pursuing this goal - sometimes we set ourselves goals to try to impress or please others. What's in it for you? What will <u>not</u> achieving this goal mean to you?

Is it important enough for you to make the effort and commitment even if the outcome falls short of your expectations? What efforts are you prepared to make? For example, wake up earlier, face fears, study, learn new skills, make new friends, even if the thought of it causes you to feel anxious, confront a situation, forgive someone, put up with an untidy house, change negative habits, etc.

What are you prepared to sacrifice - a promotion, holiday, family/leisure time, money or a guilty pleasure? How will achieving this goal benefit you and your life?

There's no truer statement than 'fail to prepare, prepare to fail.'[13] This level of enquiry should help you to set realistic goals and to help you to fine tune them.

Believe in your capacity to achieve your goal - My goal this year is to accomplish the goals of last year, which I had planned to do the previous year. Sound familiar?

We all have great intentions, dreams and hopes that we set out to achieve only to lose our way never fully accomplishing our goals. You may recall, (Chapter 2, p39) when I spoke about a condition that I call 'I can'titis' - a mental condition arising as a result of a belief choice that you make about yourself.

When you set yourself a goal, how do your beliefs stack up? Do you believe that you are deserving of this accomplishment?

Do you believe that the outcome hoped for is within the realm of possibility? Do you truly believe in your potential, ability and commitment to make this happen?

At the root of any goal stems hope, but hope and belief are intertwined. Hope means being open to the possibility of change and achievement within our life, whilst belief is more of a anchoring force giving us assurance, strength and momentum to keep on going.

I remember when I first decided on my goal to write a book, I was hopeful that it would be a great success. I had no evidence to suggest otherwise, and to be honest, I had failed to follow through on previous half-hearted attempts in the past.

In spite of that, I had a dream of writing my first book and that became my goal, which in turn became my focus. What made the real difference was my unwavering belief in me. I believed that not only did I deserve this opportunity to showcase my ability to empower and inspire others, but I had within me the capability and resources to bring this about. I truly believed in my potential to see this through.

Of course, I still had concerns and doubts around aspects of my goal, but my belief in me and my ability to do this remained strong. Despite the fact that I was beset by problems from all directions that had the potential to destroy all I had worked on, it was belief that pushed me to carry on.

If your current hopes, dreams and goals seem challenging and difficult to achieve, but are realistic for you and your ability, then you must maintain an unwavering belief that you have all that it takes to bring this change about.

Once you follow through with the assessment to help you to set relevant goals 'Belief' is then only a matter of choice.

'Whatever the Mind Can Conceive and Believe, the Mind Can Achieve'

Create your goal - It's the final piece of the jigsaw. To create anything is to bring it into existence. This is where so many people get it wrong.

"Whatever the mind can conceive and believe - the mind can achieve." This is by far one of the most famous inspirational quotes attributed to best-selling author Napolean Hill.

A few years ago, following on from a course I had attended, I decided I would put the theory of goal creation to the test. Part of the course material involved creating goals using as much sensory detail as possible. The objective was to communicate your conscious goal to the subconscious in order to bring it into existence. With that in mind I decided to really go for it and choose two goals that would certainly put the Universe to the test!

My first goal was to appear on RTE television, the flagship national station for Ireland. Of course I went about the AB stages initially, and then went about writing out my goal statement in a positive and present way. I mentally created a picture of my future, when my goal was achieved, bringing in as much detail and emotion that I could muster up.

My second goal involved public speaking, which I had never done previously. Once again I mentally placed myself to a time and place in the future, where I addressed a room full of people on the subject of Stress Management.

I practiced my visualization daily and often many times a day, as I immersed myself fully into my new future. To help me to visualise with more ease, I wrote out my goals and attached pictures and images. In this instance, I printed out the RTE Logo and attached it to my goal statement, and then I taped it to my fridge so that I would see it several times daily. As part of my goal plan, I began to develop and write out corporate wellness talks, and my husband offered to try and create a website. (He had no previous website development experience).

What happened next utterly stunned me. After a relatively short period of time and out of nowhere, I received a call from the head office of Aviva Health (previously branded as Hibernian Insurance Plc) to do a corporate talk on Work-Life Balance for one of their corporate clients in Cork. A short time after that whilst pottering about my office, I received a call from a researcher from RTE to see if I would screen test for a slot on a live television show.

Thereafter, my business began to take off, and the next couple of years involved travelling around Ireland, delivering a range of wellness talks to multi-national and international organisations with much success.

And I was blessed for having the opportunity to appear on RTE television, even though I was terrified at the time.

Get Ready To Practice Goal Setting

- Find a quiet place where you can spend 10 minutes uninterrupted.

- Choose one goal to work with.

- Close your eyes, relax, breathe slowly, drawing breath in through your nose and exhale slowly whilst intentionally relaxing the muscles within your entire body.

- Practice seeing yourself now in your mind's eye with your goal already accomplished. To help you imagine success and how you will feel, ask yourself the following questions: "How does it feel now that I have achieved my goal? What is different? What am I doing differently and with whom? What do I see, hear, taste, feel and smell? What do others notice about me, what are they saying?" After imagining your success for a few minutes or so, ask yourself, "How could I make this even better?" Now for a further remaining few minutes, imagine even greater success.

- Do this daily (ideally when you feel sleepy and are ready for bed, or first thing upon waking or both.

Remember that your subconscious cannot tell the difference between what is real or what is imagined. After a few weeks of practice, you will start to notice positive changes and opportunities that will bring you closer to your goal.

Chapter 8

Help Yourself - The 360° Life Make-Over

> **'An Ounce Of Prevention Is Worth A Pound Of Cure'**[13]

We all understand the basic concepts of self-care; eating healthy, exercising, getting enough sleep, engaging in healthy lifestyle choices, etc, however, understanding the concept does not necessarily translate to the actual practice of self-care.

No time, too busy and too tired would seem to be the current mantra for us all, as we go from one priority to another, with the promise of putting ourselves first sometime someday. All too often we give and do for others without giving and doing for ourselves, forgetting that we cannot give from a depleted source.

Life is busy, it is one big juggling act, trust me I get that. We have several routines, work and activities that we do each day, yet most are done on autopilot and as a result we seldom stop to think.

Auto-pilot is very useful for the most part, however, we can get lured into a 'doing mentality' and let life carry us along without examining whether or not we could be enjoying a healthier and better way of living. We then get stuck in a mode of complacency, going through the motions of each day, drawing from the same attitudes and behaviours even if our life is out of balance, inadequate, dull, difficult, unhappy and unhealthy.

Naturally the danger of continuing to live this way is that it will gradually wear you down and corrode all aspects of your health, happiness and wellbeing.

Domino Factor - We so often forget that our wellbeing is a combination of many areas working in harmony. The neglect of one usually impacts quite significantly on another, the domino effect if you like.

This principal is reinforced by The 'World Health Organisation,' which states that:

'Health is a state of complete physical, mental and social wellbeing and not merely the absence of disease or infirmity'.

That being said, I believe that self-care is a proactive choice and lifelong habit. It means choosing behaviours and making lifestyle choices that balances the effects of emotional and physical stress, it includes mindful eating and taking consistent positive action that also nourishes your social and spiritual wellbeing. The following self-care appraisal is an excellent tool that gives you a macro view of your life and can help you identify areas of neglect.

The 360º Life Make-Over Appraisal

This exercise is deceptively simple, yet very powerful in helping you to become acutely aware of your self-care needs. It will get you reflecting on and enquiring into the core parts that make your life what it is today, and it will enable you to pinpoint what areas need recharging and rebalancing.

When I delivered group talks around Work-Life Balance, I have seen first-hand, people who experience light bulb moments on completion of this exercise and as a result have reset their priorities.

In addition to the core self-care components of emotional, physical and social health, I have included spiritual health which I believe is of equal importance. Often when we think of spirituality, we think of it from a religious context. I see that as a traditional notion. I refer to spirituality in the context of maintaining inner peace and personal growth. Each of us has an inherent need to grow, evolve and achieve. It is fundamental to our sense of self-worth. When you begin to feel invisible and your confidence hits an all-time low, the chances are that your spiritual wellbeing is in need of nurturing.

Self-care is achieved and maintained out of knowledge and awareness. The purpose of this simple self-care appraisal is to do just that; to get you to reflect on your current life, so that you may be able to see if the gap between where you are now and where you would like to be needs rebalancing.

In essence, this exercise is intended to act like a mirror, reflecting back to you, areas of your life that have been neglected. Whilst it does not delve into every aspect of your life, or who you are as a person, it will help you to become clearer about the necessity of change within your life in order to maintain a good self-care practice.

When filling out the questionnaire overleaf, remember that honesty is of the utmost importance. It takes courage to look at your life honestly and to re-evaluate it, in order to make self-care a priority. As this exercise is for your eyes only, this should make that step a little easier.

In the following questionnaire, the answers require a simple 'yes' or 'no' – nothing between. If you find yourself in the sometimes category, tick no, for we have become masters of self-deception and the reality of sometimes may be more akin to now and then.

Are you ready?

Sit comfortably and grab a pen.

The 360° Life Make-Over Appraisal

Mental/Emotional Wellness	Yes/No
1. Do you look forward to getting up and making the most of your day?	
2. Do you read something inspiring and uplifting and or do what you love at least three times a week?	
3. Do you get your facts straight before jumping to conclusions?	
4. If you feel tired or overwhelmed do you stop to prioritise your actions?	
5. Do you say 'no' with ease if asked to do more than you feel you can handle?	
6. In a low mood? Do you do take positive action to change state instead of wallowing in self-pity?	
7. Do you frequently get adequate sleep (six to eight hours) each day?	
8. Are you your own best friend, rarely judge or criticise yourself, especially when you fail at something?	
9. Do you have a weekly planner that you schedule your priorities in? (including self-priorities)	
10. Do you rise above taking things personally?	

Physical Wellness	Yes/No
1. Are you within a normal and healthy weight as defined by you GP?	
2. Do you like your body and are you proud of it?	
3. Do you work out enough to work up a sweat at least three times weekly?	
4. Do you eat your food slowly and mindfully each time you eat?	
5. Are you a <u>non</u>-smoker?	
6. Do you regularly have blood work done to keep track of your general health (at least once a year)?	
7. Do you know what your body mass index is?	
8. Do you schedule time to support your body through stretching and relaxation exercises?	
9. Do you have consistent moderation in the quantity of your eating?	
10. Do you eat <u>less</u> than three processed meals per week? (pre-packaged foods/take-outs?)	

Spiritual Wellness	Yes/No
1. Do you take time out to relax your mind and body without distractions each day?	
2. Do you stop to acknowledge gratitude for what you have daily?	
3. Do you listen to your gut before making decisions?	
4. Do you take time out to visualise your dreams frequently?	
5. Do you know without doubt what your top 3 values are?	
6. Do you honour these values daily?	
7. Do you visit parks or places of nature and beauty regularly?	
8. Do you love what you do and do what you love?	
9. Do you have clearly written goals that you actively pursue?	
10. Are you excited about new ideas and look forward to learning, developing or challenging yourself?	

Social Wellness	Yes/No
1. Do you have someone special with whom you love and connect with?	
2. Do you hang out with positive people that support and uplift you that make you smile?	
3. Do you always treat others the way you want to be treated?	
4. Are you able to speak openly and honestly about your feelings when angry, anxious or worried?	
5. Can and do you ask for advice and or help when needed?	
6. Do you let those close to you know how much they mean to you often?	
7. Do you make time to attend family/social gatherings?	
8. Do you actively listen when others speak? (Without judgement or thinking about the next thing to say)?	
9. Can you assert yourself with ease where appropriate?	
10. Can you join into a group and communicate with ease without self-criticism and negativity?	

For each question that you answered 'yes' give yourself one point. For each question answered 'no' give yourself zero points. Each spoke on the wheel represents a number, the inside being 1 (low) to the outer spoke being 10 (high). Now total up all each of the sections and transfer the total amount for each section to the self-care wheel. So for example, if you scored 3 for your spiritual wellness and 4 for your mental wellness, as in the example below, draw a line across the dotted line as demonstrated in the diagram. There is also a blank wheel for you to fill in, once the questionnaire is completed.

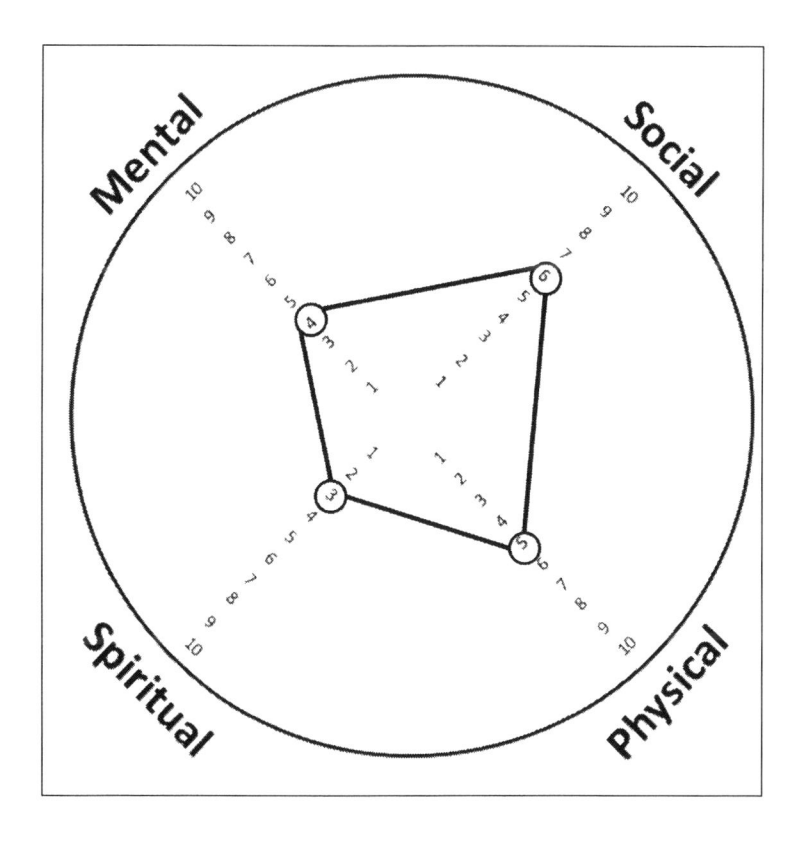

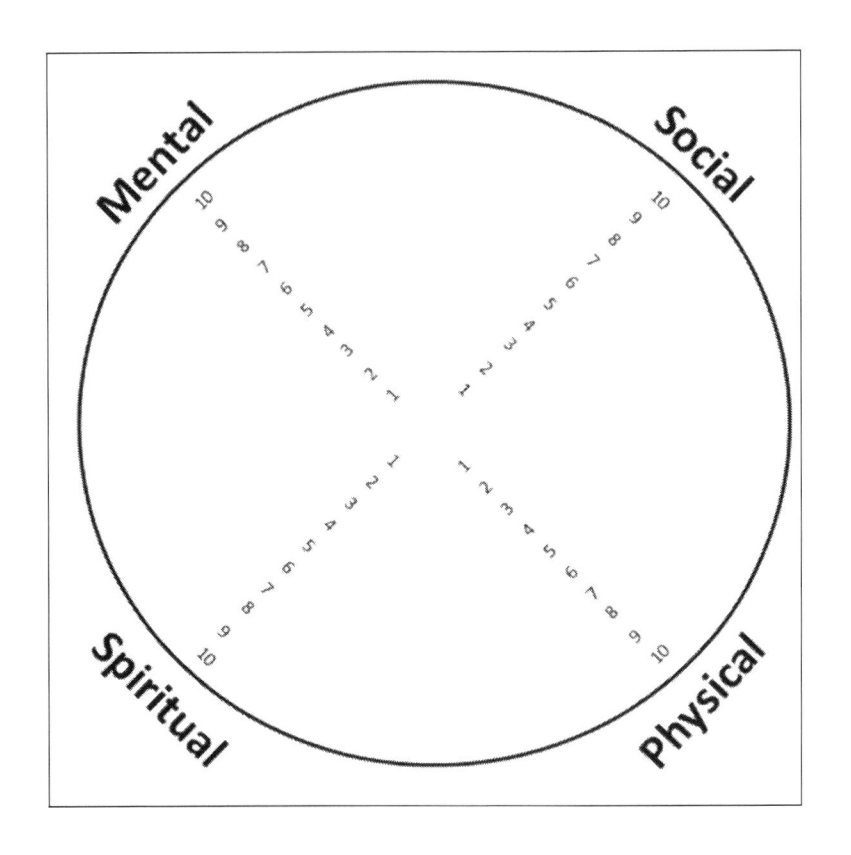

How does the picture look?

How well are you taking care of yourself?

How is your mind supporting your wellbeing?

Is your emotional environment sabotaging your physical health or relationships?

How about your physical wellbeing?

Could your diet, stress management and exercise practice do with an overhaul?

How does your social and spiritual wellness stack up?

Since most of our behaviours are driven habitually, often areas of neglect creep into our lives under the radar of our consciousness. Usually it is only when something goes wrong that we begin to re-evaluate our lives. It is for that reason, that I encourage people to do a self-care appraisal at least twice a year. It is often said that people take more care of their cars than of themselves; servicing and polishing them frequently and rarely if ever driving on a near empty tank.

Yet, how often do you run on empty? What self-care practices do you engage in consistently each week to relax and revive? Research has documented that when people don't practice self-care, they tend to experience higher rates of depression, illness, isolation and engage in self-destructive behaviours.

Now take a few minutes and ask yourself what it would mean for you to begin taking responsibility for yourself?

Self-Reflection Checklist

How might you prioritise your needs so that you can maintain the energy, drive and attitude to overcome difficulties and adversities when they do come along?

- In what ways can you improve on your physical wellbeing?

- How might you support your emotional, social and spiritual environment?

- What activities/habits could you do more of?

- Do you need to say NO more often? To whom or what, if this is the case?

- What are you not saying that you would like to say?

If you are still unclear about where to start, perhaps the following information may give you some help in devising a good self-care plan. After-all, diet and physical activity are the cornerstones of an optimal self-care practice.

Why We Get Sick

Maintaining good health and vitality is the key to any self-care plan and understanding how to best support your health is crucial. Our immune system is the foundation of good health; a simple but powerful truth. It removes toxins from our body, defends against viruses and protects us against a variety of diseases.

However, like any defence force, it requires weaponry and fuel to keep on protecting us from a host of invaders. A poor diet, stress, lack of exercise and not enough sleep all weaken our immune system. It therefore makes good sense to ensure that your plan includes healthy eating, movement and mood enhancing/relaxing activities.

Food for Thought - Much like anyone else, I do like my food and have a particular liking for Asian food with red wine and chocolate being my guilty pleasure. And over the years my curiosity for all things food has grown significantly. In many ways, I suppose you could say that I have become somewhat of a food detective in my desire to understand how foods affect our bodies.

All too often I see headlines in the media telling us of the alarming rise in a range of debilitating and life-threatening conditions that we are told are all preventative. I read about the global concern around the overuse, abuse and dependence of prescription drugs. I hear people talk about various brands of antibiotics, anti-depressants and anti-inflammatory medicine as if they had qualifications in this area. On few occasions over the years, when I felt under the weather, I have been offered prescription-strength medication by colleagues, friends or family without a visit to the doctor. Whilst the intentions are good and caring, and people's knowledge of medications are impressive, I do wonder what might happen if the same level of effort and understanding went into exploring the world of natural medicine, and by natural medicine, I refer to diet.

Don't misunderstand me, for I have enormous respect for the medical world and acknowledge the many fantastic breakthroughs and lives saved as a result of medicine. However, I often wonder how many patients leave a doctor's surgery, armed with mood altering prescriptions without other alternatives explored.

Interestingly, I stumbled upon a documentary on Channel 4 television the other day that announced that the spice saffron was as effective as some popular antidepressants in reducing depression. Some of the side effects were mood elevation and reduced appetite! However, the research is in its early stage, caution is strongly advised in terms of dosage. Just as precautions are necessary with medicine, the same rule applies for herbs and spices when medicinally used. That said, for many people suffering with depression, this could be a promising natural option without the unwelcome side-effects that come with pharmaceutical-based antidepressants.

What continually perplexes me, are the side effects associated with some medications. Of the cocktail of medication that my Dad was prescribed, one of the many side effects was that of memory impairment - how ironic, given he had dementia.

There is so much truth in the following - Ayurvedic proverb:

'When the diet is wrong, medicine is of no use, when the diet is correct, medicine is of no need'.

It is well documented that one of the best ways to fire up our immune system, lower stress, boost mood, enhance sleep and fight disease is through diet. And that being the case, you would think food science would be an obligatory subject at school. Unfortunately it's not, however, we are fortunate enough to live in an age where information is very easy to access and all you really need is a willingness to be more mindful of what and why you eat what you do.

As I was cooking the other day, I asked my youngest son Ben, "Why do you eat?" He swiftly replied, "Mum I eat to live." His reply made me chuckle a little as I quickly retorted with "Keep that in mind the next time you complain about some of the food I serve for dinner!" I then asked my eldest son Josh the same question for which he replied, "To feel good."

In truth we eat for both reasons, to live and to feel good. However, I truly believe that there is a grave imbalance around why people eat nowadays. It would seem many people the world over eat for sheer pleasure only. Whether the food eaten is packed full of nutrients or not seems irrelevant to the masses that fill up on the all too available fast and processed foods to match their fast lives.

It's not breaking news that many processed foods are unhealthy yet we continue to eat them excessively. We convince ourselves that we are too tired or have no time to cook, or that certain foods give us that shot of 'TLC' when we most need it. Whilst these foods may seem worth it at the time, the effects are short term and the reality paints a far from being worth it picture. At some level everyone knows that what we put into our mouth from day to day plays a crucial role in maintaining good health. However, I am not convinced that everyone fully grasps the complete picture of the hidden dangers lurking in our foods in general. Suffice to say, that if you often feel tired, sluggish and moody, you may find that the cause is rooted in your food choices.

Processed foods have become increasingly popular for their convenience and longevity, but the real danger lurks in their organ damaging additive ingredients. Loaded with HFCS (high fructose corn syrup), sugars, sweeteners, fake colouring, preservatives, salt and processed oils – all these ingredients cause havoc to our health and mental wellbeing. These all alluring ingredients that leave us feeling good, temporarily that is, will soon take us on a rollercoaster of highs and lows, leaving us feeling flat, moody, inactive and lethargic.

Indeed there are several published studies that provide clear evidence of the link between sugar consumption, refined oils, refined grains and many other artificial ingredients, to a whole range of illnesses and diseases including and not limited to, heart disease, type 2 diabetes, allergies and metabolic syndrome.

How, you may wonder?

It would seem that we have become guinea pigs for food science experiments. These ingredients are largely man-made and are far from natural or nutritious. Take vegetable oils, for example. If you're like me you would innocently assume that vegetable oils are healthy, right? After-all the oil is extracted from a vegetable.

Wrong assumption, as all is not what is seems.

To get oil from its source, it first must be extracted and cleaned and unfortunately many food companies use heat, chemicals and bleach in this process, which as it turns out causes the oil to go rancid. Of particular concern are oils that have been hydrogenated; also known as trans-fats, this process alters their chemical structure converting them to trans-fat.

Now I don't want to bamboozle you with chemical science, but so nasty are these fats that in 2003, I read that Denmark put a ban on the sale of products containing trans-fats with many other countries taking action to significantly reduce or eliminate them from diets.

The 'WHO' (World Health Organisation) regional committee for Europe stated in 2014:

"Consumption of trans-fats is strongly associated with an increased risk of cardiovascular disease and has been linked to several types of cancer. A growing number of countries in the 'WHO' European region have recognised that taking action to eliminate trans-fats may bring significant health gains."

Trans-fat is considered by the medical profession to be the worst type of fat you can eat. Yet, it is found in multiple food products stacked high in the supermarket aisles, in fast food outlets and in many restaurants. Used by so many because these cheap oils serve a purpose – they give products a longer shelf life, and for the fast food outlet and restaurateurs, it means their deep fat fryers don't have to be changed as often. Yuk! This sends a clear message that profits are being put before our health.

One of the most commonly ordered side at a restaurant is fries on the side. 'Fish n Chips' is another popular take out for those too tired to cook. An afternoon catch up at a cafe with a friend usually includes a cake or cookie to go with the latte. And all the while these not so innocent dishes all contain dangerous trans-fats. Even consumed at low levels, studies warn of their dangers.

And if that wasn't enough to get you rethinking your diet, some of these very same ingredients stimulate the reward centre of the brain thereby making us crave more, turning us into junk-food addicts.

A startling example of this was seen when a college in Connecticut, America, did a study in 2013 on rats fed with a well known brand of cookie. The study was designed to explore the potential addictiveness of high-fat/high-sugar foods. What came to light was this - the rats fed with cookies formed an equally strong association with the cookies, comparable to those fed with morphine or cocaine. They also found that the rats eating cookies activated more neurons in the brain's 'pleasure centre' than exposure to the drugs. This clearly shows the connection to the idea that unhealthy fat/sugar foods can be addictive. Perhaps this study may lend itself to further studies that may finally hammer home the message of the dangers of most processed foods.

We are acutely aware of the health hazards of drug abuse, but it seems that many people underestimate the effect of their diet on their mental and physical wellbeing. I often hear people say healthy eating can be hard work and that life is for living. There is a great irony in that statement. To live life to the full requires vitality and good health. To continue to consume excess bad fats and high levels of refined sugars comes at a cost.

Health is a precious gift and once you lose it, it can be difficult to restore.

I myself am work in progress in this area, as I endeavour to continue on in my journey to reduce my indulgences – and yes, I know it is not an easy feat, but it is possible to outsmart these products by becoming more food savvy through self-regulation and an awareness of the types of foods that harm to those that heal. Labels and the marketing of these foods can also be misleading as food manufacturers dream up more creative ways to label and sell their products.

The best advice that I can give you is to forget about all the fancy packaging, ignore the marketing jargon and go straight to the nutritional label, which is never made easy for us to read as it's usually printed in such small print that a magnifying glass may be in order to decipher its content. And if you're about to head down the low fat/non fat route as a result of all that talk about dangerous fats, think again. Not all fats are made equal, and in fact a low fat/non fat diet can actually make you fat.

Today, most supermarket shelves are stacked high with non fat/low fat products, which is in total contrast from the fat rich diets of our parents and grandparents generation. You may already be aware that saturated fat became vilified a few decades ago due to the connection between elevated cholesterol and heart disease. As a result low fat/non fat products became standard recommendation.

Typical advice was to substitute real butter for soft tub spreads, cook with vegetable oils, select dairy products made with 'low' or 'no' fat, and eggs were bad. Yet are we healthier as a result? According to the World Health Organization, heart disease remains the leading cause of death in the world and diabetes continues to rise as is obesity. And now after many years of the medical establishments convincing us to avoid saturated fats, it would appear that some are now beginning to acknowledge that they may have got this wrong. For example, I continue to read several online articles from established sources that suggest that many medical professionals and leading cardiologists are now in agreement that saturated fats and dietary cholesterol have no bearing on heart disease. Does this then mean that animal fats, eggs, butter, full fat dairy and cooking oils such as coconut oil are back on the menu?

It would appear so.

Eat fat and get thin, appears to be the new message.

Take the humble avocado. Avocados are mainly fat, with roughly 77% of its energy coming from fat. Yet despite being high in fat, there are several studies that suggest that people who eat avocados tend to weigh less and have less belly fat than those who don't. The link in weight loss is due to the high fat content and its ability to stabilise blood sugar levels, help you feel full faster, which in turn staves off cravings and hunger pangs. Boasting more potassium that a banana, avocadoes are also high in antioxidants that support the liver to filter out toxins from the body. And if that's not enough to get you eating them, avocadoes are rich in B vitamins, which naturally lower stress level, making them an excellent food for good self-care practice.

I now eat half an avocado at least 4 days a week, a handful of almond nuts daily and I cook with organic, cold pressed, unrefined coconut oil. I do like fish, though I supplement with Omega 3 oil that includes squid and calamari oil. My point is this: do not be afraid of fat, as not all fat is equal. Source natural unprocessed, organic fats in combination with a diet, that is free of or very low in trans-fats and refined sugars. Eat as much fresh vegetables particularly the green leafy kind, and use sweet potatoes in place of regular potatoes often.

Remember getting hooked on poor eating habits did not happen overnight. It's about creating new habits which will take time, so be patient and expect to experience some level of discomfort and frustration. As I've said, I am still working on creating new habits and yes I do stumble and take steps back, but I remain mindful and that keeps me moving forward.

Balance really is the key; choosing to eat less processed foods and more natural foods fresh from the ground and ocean is a great place to start.

Let's Get Physical

Have you ever noticed the more stress you are experiencing, the less inclined you are to want to get up and move. Yet, it has been proven time and time again, that physical activity is not just good for you, it is a necessity, even more so when you are feeling dispirited and discouraged. Getting up and being active has enormous and profound benefits, not only for your heart, lungs, brain, muscles and bones, but by just moving, you activate your brain to release endorphins (happy hormones), which gives you a big mood boost and increased energy.

So there you have it, there is no disputing the powerful effect that exercise has on our immune system and emotional health. That said, why then can it be difficult for people to maintain a regular routine of activity given the undisputed benefits that it brings?

If I had a euro for all the times I hear people complain that they wish they had more time to do exercise, I would have a very healthy bank account. Yet these very same people often squander precious time zoned out in front of the television numbing their minds with the latest slice of drama and chaos that modern television has on offer today. The biggest thieves of our time are usually screen based. Whether it's television, laptop or mobile, the harsh reality is that people have become so habitually addicted to screen entertainment in whatever guise that is, they 'think' that they do not have enough time.

The reality is that, each and every one of us has the same equal time. Please understand that time or the perceived lack of it, is not the enemy.

Time Thieves and Time Guardians - The real enemy of our time is what I call 'time thieves' and getting clear on precisely what your 'time thieves' are is a good starting point.

For point of clarity 'time thieves' are people or things that consume large amounts of your time, especially without achieving anything productive.

The table opposite, gives some examples of typical 'time thieves' along with corresponding ideas to help you protect your time and manage your energy more effectively. I like to call these 'time guardians.' You may have additional 'time thieves' too, so feel free to add to the list.

Times Thieves	Time Guardians
Inactivity	Physical Activity
Stress	Relaxation
Procrastination	Pro-Activity
Distractions/interruptions	Personal Boundaries

The stark reality is that most of our days are filled with many great opportunities to experience a more fulfilled life, but go wasted because our focus and attention is drawn elsewhere. Think of all the time you have squandered and opportunities wasted as a result of being too tired, too stressed, procrastinating, being a people pleaser or being disorganised? Let's look at the time thieves more closely.

Stress and physical inactivity tend to go unnoticed as time wasters, yet both cause people to lack focus, impair decision-making ability and create emotional instability, all of which does not make for a productive person.

I would also say that a significant amount of people's time is consumed as a result of stress-related illness and general un-wellness.

Yet, if people were to truly make the best use of their time, finding ways to calm down, relax and instilling a weekly habit of physical activity would be an absolute non-negotiable priority.

So where does it go wrong?

Why is it that so many people say that they have a clear picture of what is important to them, such as their health for example, yet exercise does not make it on their weekly schedule?

My guess is that when you've had a long demanding day, or anticipate a hard slog ahead, it's easy to feel tired and overwhelmed, and the last thing you want to feel is anymore stress or pressure, so you try to find an escape route. You know you 'should' be doing other things, but you just can't bring yourself to do them, even if you know they would be of benefit to you.

So you watch TV, you surf the net, you interact on social media, raid the fridge and guzzle down a beer or wine.

Do you feel any better? Of course you do, short term, and then the heavy hand of guilt weighs down on your already fatigued mind, particularly if done all too often. You then think "What's wrong with me, I wish I were somewhere else, I just can't switch off and relax, It's easier said than done, I am not disciplined enough," etc.

Let me tell you now that these feelings are normal, so don't go beating yourself up, however that said, nothing will change unless you do something positive to change this merry go round of wishing you did not feel the way you do. Feeling better and re-prioritizing can only happen once you become 'Proactive' (a favourite 'time guardian' of mine). And just to be clear, proactive is defined as creating or controlling a situation rather than just reacting to it after it has happened.

Simply put, you and you alone can make things happen instead of waiting for them to happen to you.

Can you recall in Chapter 2 when I said: "Caught up in a survival mentality can do one of two things to a person. It can lure you into a state of powerlessness and helplessness, or it can make you enterprising, resourceful and even more determined to reach your dreams." That is what I mean about being proactive.

There are few things in life that we can control and unless you have a grave disability that restricts your movement, physical exercise is one such thing that we have total control over. The power literally lies within you. Unless you take conscious control of allocating time for your personal priorities, others will allocate your time for themselves. Richard Branson, one of the world's most successful and respected entrepreneur is noted for saying, that staying physically active is key to his productivity.

Think of it like this, every single action you take each day, however small will determine the person you are tomorrow. What person are you becoming? If happiness, longevity and vitality are important values to you, then physical activity, done consistently each week must become one of your non-negotiable personal rituals. A good way to galvanise yourself into action and attend to your self-care rituals is to map them out onto out a weekly 'time planner'.

Think about it this way, you schedule appointments and meetings of all descriptions from doctor, dentist and school appointments to work related meetings, so why not schedule meetings with yourself? This will enable you to assign specific times for your self-care needs including your physical activities. Ideally, make this the same time every week so that it becomes an automated practice, just as brushing your teeth and other such practices have become a daily/weekly ritual.

Once you have brainstormed a list of activities, be sure to choose an activity that you enjoy doing and offers some level of challenge to give you the added sense of achievement. Change your activities and self-care rituals around from time to time too, to keep things new and fresh.

I usually aim to do my exercise activity in the mornings and committing to an earlier wake up time is sometimes necessary to ensure that value is honoured. Once established as a regular routine, your life will take on a new lease of life and vigour, for which you will have more energy and time to do all those other things that need doing.

It warrants saying again, any activity is positive and highly beneficial because it:

- Decreases the production of stress hormones.

- Induces the relaxation response, pumps up your endorphins, increases energy levels and lowers symptoms associated with anxiety and depression.

- Motivational – The more you do the more you want to do, which in turn increases confidence and self-esteem.

Procrastination

The art of not getting done what really needs to be done.

For me this is by far a very sneaky 'time thief' because it fools you into thinking that you are busy, when it fact a busy fool might be a more accurate description. It's very easy to get pulled into many different directions and tasks to do, with so many people and things competing for your time. The problem with being drawn into this doing mode is that you end up reacting to a whole lot of interruptions and requests, which usually don't contribute to what really needs to get done. We do this for all sorts of reasons, especially when the thing to be done is tedious and unexciting, or it feels too challenging or involves making an effort. So these things remain on the "I will do it soon list" which grows longer by the week.

Learning to distinguish between what should and must be done is a useful way to cut through your to-do list. Ask yourself if each item on your to-do list is really relevant and consistent with your priorities for that week/month? Often things end up on our to-do list because we feel we 'should' do it. You may recall 'uncovering blind spots' in (Chapter 5) and how we need to watch out for the 'shoulds'. If 'shoulds' show up on your 'to do' list, take heed, as they usually end up there out of guilt because of our need to be liked, and we don't like to let people down.

I tend to use the 4D approach to sorting through my to-do list. I came across it years ago, and it offers a very simple and practical approach to getting things done.

Do it	Diary it
Delegate it	Dump it

Use the following criteria to help you decide where to assign it. Ask yourself the following:

- Is it important and urgent?

- What are the consequences of **not** getting it done that day/week?

- Can it be scheduled to a near date in the future?

- Can I hand this over to someone else to be done?

- By saying yes to including this item on my to-do list, what or who am I saying no to?

- Is this task coherent to my life/business priorities or just a time waster?

We get sidetracked by so many distractions, demands and interruptions, that we often lose our sense of direction in the process. Sometimes we get caught up doing things that are less urgent because we buy into other people's dramas, or because they shout the loudest. The core function of this approach is to simply help you to consciously distinguish between time wasters and important tasks, from those that can be scheduled or shared.

Personal Boundaries

Protecting yourself from Time and Energy Vampires

Do you feel that people take advantage of you? Perhaps you find yourself doing things that you don't want or need to do? Maybe you have been overdoing it and not getting enough down time? If this resonates with you, the chances' are that you may need to revisit your personal boundaries.

It's a term I don't often hear people use, yet it is of significant value in protecting your precious time and energy from what I call time vampires and in some cases energy vampires, as I believe they are closely related. These people appear everywhere, be it at work, socially or within the family circle. They can be demanding, needy, critical and negative. Personal boundaries are defined as 'guidelines, rules or limits that a person creates to identify reasonable, safe and permissible ways for other people to behave towards him or her and how he/she will respond when someone passes those limits.'

In simple terms, they act like invisible barriers that we put up to prevent us from being manipulated, taken advantage of, or feel disrespected by others. Your relationship with yourself is one of the most important relationships that you will have in this lifetime, and when you are unhappy not only will that relationship suffer, but relationships with others will also come under strain.

Think about the times when you have felt resentful, annoyed or guilty as a result of another's expectation, request or demand of you. That is why establishing healthy boundaries are important; they make for better quality relationships and nourish self-esteem, whilst protecting your most precious resources, your time and energy.

The following are indicators that you have poorly set boundaries in place:

- Often feeling guilty when you turn down a request.

- Doing things you'd rather not do, just to please or be perceived as good or useful.

- Not voicing your opinion when you have something valid to say.

- Becoming too emotionally involved in other's dramas.

- Not holding someone accountable who mistreats you.

- Frequently allow yourself to be interrupted to accommodate other people's needs or demands.

We sometimes fall into a pattern of people pleasing, that others often and unintentionally take advantage of. However, that's not to suggest that you create rigid boundaries. Healthy boundaries promote mutual respect and encourage a give and take relationship.

It's not about being inflexible or bossy. There will be many times in which you will chose to lower the barriers of your boundaries, particularly if someone needs additional support, help, understanding and love, as we all do many times throughout our lives. The point of implementing boundaries is to empower you to recognise that your time and energy is as valuable as everyone else. So when you do encounter the self-absorbed, aggressive, highly critical, demanding or needy people, you will know how to respond rather than feel intimidated.

When to say 'Yes' - When to say 'No'

How to Redefine Your Boundaries

Boundaries are very personal, and you alone are the only person that will know how much of you and your time you want to give to others, which will no doubt vary from time to time depending on what is going on within your own life. A good place to start is to define your values – those things that really matter most to you.

So for example, if family is a core value, yet the amount of quality time spent with them is frequently compromised, it would make sense to make a note of the situations and people that you have allowed to take advantage. Perhaps you're giving too much of your time in one area or to a particular person at the consequence of another. Maybe you have been putting up with situations that you no longer find fair, reasonable or fulfilling. I recall some years back, a friend of mine needed a large amount of my attention by way of social and emotional support, for which I was happy to give. As time moved on and our paths moved in different directions, what became transparent was this – that person rarely connected in with me, knew nothing of my difficulties yet out of the blue would expect me to drop everything to offer my advice and help, despite not hearing a whisper from her from one year to the next.

I found myself drained, with my energy and time depleted on the occasions that I allowed myself to become available to her. When I finally asserted that I was busy with other things going on (and believe me there were things coming at me in all directions at the time) and that I was not in a position to help out in that moment, I never heard from her again!

What I have observed especially in my work is that relationships that are worthwhile, valuable and authentic are not broken as a result of your boundaries. People often say that they can't assert themselves particularly if a person perceives an imbalance of power, i.e. your manager, teacher, parent, etc. Please understand that you have a right to an opinion, a right to state your point of view, a right to be treated with respect and dignity, and a right to defer people or to negotiate a compromise at whatever age or stage you are at in life.

I believe that many times people who make demands of you which may seem unfair are as a result of conflicting values, i.e. your manger's demands may be driven by career advancement conflicting with your family time value. Often there is no ill will, just a conflict of ideas or values. Which is why communicating your boundaries by way of developing your ability to assert yourself is an important life skill. Some people experience difficulty in communicating their boundaries and if that rings true for you, what might be lurking in the background are emotional barriers.

Emotional barriers are usually fears, self-doubts, mistrust and suspicion, which can all stunt our ability to communicate our feelings in an open and honest way. As the diagram illustrates, many of these emotions are rooted in the past from previous experiences, which in turn causes us to avoid speaking our truth.

Emotional Barriers

⬇

Fear

Suspicion — Rooted In the Past — **Mistrust**

Self Doubt

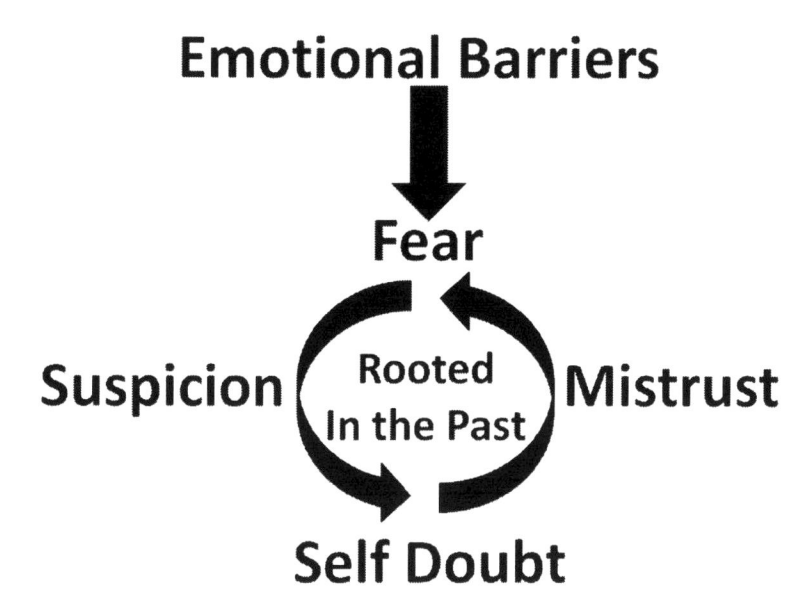

To coin the phrase, 'We don't see things as they are we see them as we are.'[21] Our preconceptions have the power to dramatically alter the way we perceive people and situations, and as a result our emotional barriers will often get in our way.

Once you understand your rights, acknowledge that you matter and recognise any barriers for what they are, you free yourself to communicate assertively. Be careful, some people confuse assertive behaviour with aggressive or manipulative behaviour. Healthy well-meant, assertive behaviour means expressing yourself in an honest and appropriate way that 'also' respects the views, opinions and needs of the person/people that you are communicating with.

Of equal importance is that assertiveness is influenced by 'what is right' and not about 'being right'.

Chapter 9

Using Empathy For Better Relationships

> **'Instead of putting others in their place, put yourself in their place'**[14]

It may be the final characteristic in 'System Pause,' but it is the most profound. Imagine what it is like to step outside of your own feelings momentarily and experience things from another person's viewpoint - that in principal is what is called empathy. It's the ability to put ourselves into another person's shoes, so that we can better connect with another and understand their feelings and motivations.

Why is that important you may wonder? Being socially engaged is the life force to personal resilience, and being able to empathise is an extremely vital component to developing and maintaining positive relationships. All too often we misunderstand others and we are quick to make judgement, just as others misunderstand and judge us, and as a result relationships breakdown and we may feel isolated and alone. Being human we are conditioned to interact socially, therefore the ability to form healthy relationships is paramount to our happiness and wellbeing.

Now I realise that many of you might be thinking that being socially active is not as easy as it sounds, and trust me I know that all too well from experience. Feeling left out and alone can come along at different times throughout our lives, and for me it started when I had moved to Australia and these feelings heightened significantly upon my return to London, when I decided to try and re-invent my life. Despite working in London and being surrounded by many lovely work colleagues, most of my evenings and weekends were spent alone, and I found myself craving for nights out and an opportunity to get back on the romantic scene.

At the time I had lived on the outskirts of London, which added to the challenges of staying socially connected. On the occasions when I did muster up the courage to dine out for lunch on my own, it was never made any easier by the waiter who would announce, "Oh you're on your own," as he swiftly reset the table for one. As I watched couples and groups revelling in chat and laughter, my heart knew something had to change. Despite my anxieties around trying to connect with new people, I knew it was down to me. I knew I had to take positive action.

With my 'more to gain' mindset I hatched a plan.

With a piece of paper in one hand and a pen in the other, I decided I would start up a social network group, and with that I placed an advertisement in the newspaper. The strap-line went something along the lines of: "Tired of watching Jerry Springer? Why not join an-all-girl's social-network that meet weekly to trip the light fantastic."

That was my plan. I now had to wait and see who would respond, and if this social group was to become a reality. I had no idea what to expect, as I had never organised anything bigger than a night out with my two sisters, nor did I know what shape this social group would take. It wasn't long before several girls responded, many who found themselves in similar circumstances as mine. The reality is that social disconnect touches all our lives at some point; relationships end, friends move away, some have babies, others get caught up in their businesses/jobs, and before we know it, we find ourselves alone. That day, had I not took a proactive approach to change my situation, I would have remained socially disconnected.

I see empathy as the key to opening the social door to enable our relationships to flourish. And you don't have to take my word for it. Much research has been done on the importance of this highly valued trait and some of the benefits that are associated with an increase in empathy include

- A reduction in reactive behaviour.

- Enhanced friendships and intimate relationships.

- Better communication.

- Healthy self-esteem.

- General happiness and wellbeing.

Our ability to be empathic can help us to remain open, defuse conflict, build trust, and prevent us from taking things personally. If you have been blessed to have been on the receiving end of true empathy, you will then appreciate the deep sense of feeling understood and of being supported. I can honestly say that without the true empathy shown to me throughout the years by a special few people, I am not sure I would be the same person today as I am now. When you hit the downward run on life's rollercoaster, it is not only a terrifying time, but a time when you feel at your most vulnerable. Knowing that you can call on someone, who can see your faults and failings without judgement, who can hear your feelings even when no words have been spoken, is a very comforting experience. Without a shadow of doubt, I believe that we can all rise above the smothering effects of adversities when we share the company of others that connect with us empathically.

I believe that each of us are born with a natural capacity to empathise, which is why we can share the moments of happiness with loved ones and feel the frustration and pain of those who are aggrieved. However, I also think that there are times when our empathy tank runs low, and if left unchecked, can alienate us from others, and cause us to feel disconnected and alone.

Although I am not an expert on the subject of empathy, I would consider myself to be on the higher end of the empathy continuum scale, and have come to learn and understand some of the blocks that get in the way from utilizing our empathy muscles to their fullest potential. I believe these to be stress, anger, poor communication and technology.

Ways to Increase Empathy to Optimise Your Relationships

Practice Mindfulness - When we are going through our own stress and turmoil, it can be easy to get caught up to the point where our sense of empathy is closed off. Let's be honest, how often have you felt less receptive to the needs and plight of others after a long hard day, and more so when there is a differing of opinions or clash of values apparent. There is no doubt about it, stress weakens our empathy muscles, and you may find yourself slipping into the 'everyone for themselves' mindset with little tolerance for anyone else. That's not to say that you are inherently an insensitive person. When we are pulled in several different directions and left feeling drained from clambering through the day, it is easy to lose touch with the core value of empathy.

If this is true for you, then taking personal responsibility to increase your empathy tank is crucial. People who lack the capacity or desire to show empathy to others, more often experience difficult relationships that lack depth, closeness and meaning. Cultivating mindfulness is one approach to developing empathy, and has the remarkable effect of lowering anxiety and stress at the same time. Mindfulness teaches us to stand back from ourselves and notice our thoughts, people and things without criticism. When practiced often, this non-judgemental approach helps us let go of emotional reactivity, which in turn paves the way for compassion to shine through. In a nutshell, that's what mindfulness is and there are several books, courses and on line resources that can help you get started. To give you a flavour of the basics try the following one minute mindfulness exercise.

This exercise can be done anywhere at any time, though best done seated if you are new to the concept. You will already have practiced breath work in part one of 'System Pause,' so you should now begin to realise, just how powerful an impact our breathing has over our lives in general.

A one-minute Mindfulness Meditation

1. Set your alarm for one minute. Close or lower your eyes towards the ground.

2. Without altering your natural breathing rhythm, bring your focus to your breath, as it flows in and out of your body. Purposefully bring your attention to any sensations that you notice, as you inhale and exhale.

3. Should you find that your mind has wandered off, which it no doubt will, simply bring your attention back to your breath.

4. If you feel critical of yourself or you feel you can't concentrate on your breath for long, let those thoughts be as they are. Don't struggle with this inner chatter, just once again bring your focus and attention back to your breath, following the sensation of the air as you inhale and exhale.

5. After one minute, open your eyes and bring your focus back into the room.

How did you feel?

Indifferent, calm, bored or even frustrated?

You may have felt relaxed momentarily and lost it again. This is all perfectly normal.

The key to mindfulness is noticing when your mind starts to wander off and being with your thoughts as they come to mind, and letting go of any urge to engage with them. With practice, and practice you must if you are to get the hang of this, it does get easier, and you will come to understand that your thoughts don't have to control you.

In fact, all your thoughts can be short lived as they are in a constant state of flux. As you become more practiced, you will begin to understand that your thoughts do disappear just as quickly as they appear, and that you don't have to be at the mercy of your mind chatter, which will help put you back in control of your life.

I once read that someone asked Buddha:

"What have you gained through meditation?" to which Buddha replied;

"Nothing at all", and then went on to say: "Let me tell you what I lost through meditation - sickness, anger, insecurity, the burden of old age and the fear of death."

There exists numerous studies worldwide that have proven that meditation, if practiced regularly, reduces stress, anxiety, irritability and depression, to name but a few. In fact, those that meditate regularly, not only have better immune systems, but enjoy better quality relationships and are usually more compassionate.

Practice Better Communication Skills

We cannot, not communicate. That's a fact. We are communicating all of the time even when no words are spoken, a fact that is often overlooked because we are so used to the spoken word. Yet, surprisingly, it is suggested that our words only constitute 7% of our total communication, as you will see from the illustration below.

And with the continuous advances in technology, likely designed in order to make our lives move even faster, is it any wonder that our empathy muscles have grown weaker? With less time spent with people in the physical form, these communication short cuts make it even more difficult to read and understand how another person may truly be feeling. Don't get me wrong, I do get the benefits of virtual communication however I do wonder, if too many people are becoming increasingly reliant on the online world of communication in place of physical connectedness.

Non Verbal Communication

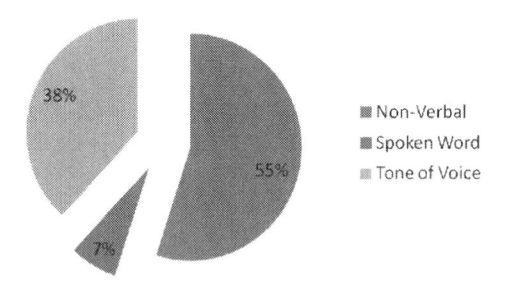

- Non-Verbal — 55%
- Spoken Word — 7%
- Tone of Voice — 38%

The other day at my local restaurant, the owner was sharing her concerns around the amount of people that she observes daily that come out for dinner, only to spend the entire time on their screens/mobiles. These include couples and families who I presume have come out to spend quality time with each other. The irony!

Communicating well is not just a goal to aspire to, it's more than that, its' an essential life skill that is integral to increasing and maintaining empathy. With a little insight, self-knowledge and effort, it is possible to improve your communication effectiveness.

Social style awareness is a good place to start and there are plenty resources that you can access, which will give you an excellent introduction. Typically used by hundreds of organisations worldwide, this simple but highly valuable tool can provide you with insights' that can help you to identify and understand the behavioural tendencies and habits of others including yourself. To help you along the way, let me give you a brief overview from my understanding and research.

Developed in the 1960s by Dr. David Merrill and Roger Reid, it is proposed that there are four unique social styles, of which we all have our own dominant style. In other words, the manner of talking and behaving with which we become habitually used to and comfortable with.

Most of us have no clue as to how we come across to others, and often when we struggle with getting along with others it is most likely as a result of them having a differing social style from us, rather than them being deliberately awkward, wrong or distant.

No one style is greater than the other and learning to understand the strengths and perceived weaknesses of each style, can be of enormous value for nurturing empathy and maintaining satisfying relationships.

As you can see from the diagram to follow, the horizontal axis describes assertiveness, running along a continuum of low to high assertiveness. The vertical axis represents responsiveness, which essentially means the degree in which a person shows and shares their emotions and feelings. Those social styles that fall on the low responsive side are usually less expressive about their feelings/emotions, they show less gestures, when communicating, tend not to engage in small talk, are typically task driven with decisions being primarily made based on hard facts and data.

On the other hand, those on the high responsive continuum are more animated and expressive when communicating, are people orientated making them more socially inclined and are more often open to sharing their feelings/emotions. Decisions made are typically gut/intuition based or are influenced by what others think.

The social styles on the low assertiveness continuum are more 'ask' rather than 'tell' orientated, take less risks, are less confrontational, less decisive, and are usually more gently spoken with slower movement. Conversely, the styles on the high assertive tend to be more outspoken and direct orientated, decisive, can be more confrontational and are recognised by fast action/movement.

Analytical Social Style - From that it can be summarised that an analytical social style is positioned along the low responsive/low assertiveness scale. Based on this theory, this social style can be perceived by others as uncommunicative, aloof and stand-offish. They are also considered prudent, shrewd, reserved and logical, and the 'thinkers' of the four styles. They are detail driven and much of their decision making is based on hard facts, which is why they do not like to be rushed into things. Under stress, an analytical may withdraw to avoid conflict.

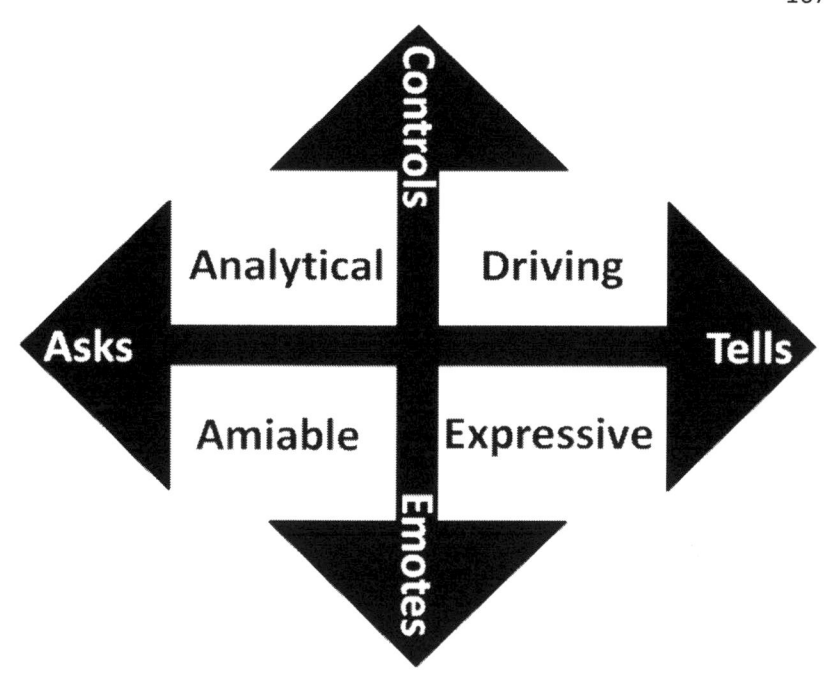

Driver Social Style – Much like the analytical, the driver also sits on the low responsive, suggesting that they too do not show their feelings/emotions easily. Logical in their approach, their decisions are also based on hard facts and data. Unlike the analytical, drivers are on the high end of the assertive axis, meaning that they are more likely to be directive and outspoken in their approach when dealing with people, and can easily assume control of situations.

Persuasive, determined, competitive and independent, drivers do not shy away from confrontation. As a result, they can be perceived as inconsiderate and bossy. As high achievers, this social style is less tolerant of small talk and of perceived time wasting activities. Under stressful conditions this social style can resort to being domineering, taking no account of other's needs or opinions.

Amiable Social Style – Positioned on the high responsive/low assertiveness axis, this social style is one of the most accommodating of the four styles. Personable, patient and cooperative, amiable styles are openly expressive about their feelings. They place a high value on relationships and acceptance is important to them. Unlike the driver, this social style is inclined to engage in small talk given that building rapport with others is important to them. Not big on risk-taking, much of their decision making is typically influenced by others thoughts and opinions. Under stress the amiable has a tendency to be submissive.

Expressive Social Style – Like the amiable, this social style places high value on relationships and like the director style, is opinionated, competitive and fast paced, and equally does not shy away from risk-taking. The expressive social style person is people orientated, is great at motivating others and has strong social capability. This style can be impulsive with little concern for details and facts. Perceived by others as approachable, energetic, inspiring, hasty and dramatic, and when stressed, the expressive may have a tendency to go on the personal attack.

Now perhaps, you are thinking that you fit more than one profile, I know I certainly do. However, it is said that each of us do lean towards a dominant style that we fundamentally function from, during our interactions with others. Therefore it's about the consistent patterns of behaviour that we exhibit when we are in the company of others. In short, if you are continuing to struggle in some way with others at work and or personally, this framework could be just what you need to improve your relationships going forward, whilst helping you to cultivate more empathy.

All too often, we are quick to point the finger and make judgements, but by realizing that each of us have differing styles of communicating with each other, can you then begin to grow.

The primary benefit of learning about social styles is the insight for which this knowledge provides for communicating better with others. Once you begin honing these skills you will find it easier to deal with the fragilities and shortcomings of others.

Always worth remembering, is that regardless of how different each of us are, the one thing that all of us have in common is that of life - we are all connected in one way or another with core basic needs that drive us. Most of us simply want to belong, to feel safe and secure, to be loved, understood, appreciated and acknowledged, and to feel that someone is there to lend us a shoulder or helping hand when we face tough times.

P → Positive
A → Acceptance
U → Undeterred
S → Self - Care
E → Empathy

BREATHE

Case Studies

To illustrate aspects of System Pause at work, let me tell you about some of my clients that have come to me for personal coaching. We will begin with a person that I will call John, who came to me because he felt his life was out of balance.

John

John is a happily married father of three children, has a well paid job, is mortgage free and is financially secure. Yet despite his outward successes, John felt emotionally overwhelmed. This manifested as general anxiety; excess feelings of negativity, breathlessness, nausea, worry etc. His job carried a lot of responsibility and deadlines, and additionally, he was under increasing pressure to reach ever changing targets. He felt consumed by work demands, and guilty for not spending enough quality time with the family. Of the little free time that John did have, he felt too tired to do anything of significance, which led to him feeling even more self-critical.

We took a look at his self-care wheel which brought about a renewed sense of clarity. With little to no self-care and stress management practices in place, it was no wonder that John felt emotionally overwhelmed. As we began to discuss each area on the self-care wheel, we uncovered a crucial factor. John feared not being 'good enough'. As a result, everything he did was driven by achievement, which hinged on perfectionism.

I asked John to explain how he would know, when 'good enough was'. I wanted to know what yardstick he used to measure this. He had never really given this concept much thought, yet his mind was consumed frequently, by feelings of not being good enough. On reflection, John revealed that being 'good enough,' was largely reliant on other's appraisal of him. As a result he craved reassurance frequently, which meant that he was on an emotional rollercoaster of highs and lows, dependent on the situation he found himself in, and on how others felt towards him.

The concept of self-validation, along with stress management was discussed, and as a result John set about devising new goals that supported his sense of self-power and self-worth. John went about constructing a self-supporting system, something that had never occurred to him previously. He began a 'thought journal' that enabled him to reframe his thinking, which helped him to understand and overcome any negative and reactive thoughts. He integrated deep breathing daily to help him regain a sense of calm and control. He devised his own 'personal strengths inventory', along with the integration of a daily 'gratitude journal.' With practice, he began to see how self-validation was a far better way to nourish his self-worth. As John began to experience a sense of personal power, he felt more energised and positive. This was reflected in his appetite to experience more leisure time with his wife and children.

We all go through times where we lose our self-worth, particularly when we encounter experiences where we are ignored, criticised or rejected. Whilst seeking validation from other people has its benefits, we spend far too much of our time and energy leaning on this approach to feel better about ourselves. However, when we regularly acknowledge our strengths and value, self-love and self-acceptance becomes a habit. As long as we breathe, we will continue to encounter experiences that will shake the basis of our self-worth. As we move through life, our inner critic will continue to hitch a ride within our mind, therefore it is crucial that we have at the very least, a self-supporting system that depends less on validation from others and more on self-validation.

Marie

Marie is a mum of three young children and had experienced much of the drama and chaos that comes with motherhood. She came to me for coaching because she felt stuck. She felt that she lost her direction in life, and that a part of her seemed to be missing. Eager to be nice and to please others, she found it hard to say no and as a result, Marie had slipped into a negative state of mind, where she experienced frequent bouts of resentment, anger, sadness and guilt.

Prior to her children she had worked full time and enjoyed being socially active. She had found it hard to lose the added weight she gained during her pregnancies, which further fuelled her self-loathing. She described her life, as if she were on a hamster wheel, going around in endless circles.

Sitting opposite Marie, I could see that her posture was tense and her breathing was anxious. She presented as if she was carrying the world on her shoulders. When I asked her what she did to relax, she said that she can't relax, that she found it difficult to sit still and that her mind raced with too many things, which prevented her from unwinding. I then proceeded to talk her through a two minute breathing cycle, which brought her into an immediate calmer state.

Being able to 'Pause for Breath', in those two minutes gave Marie a momentary sense of calm, and where she felt more in control. That was the first step of her awareness journey, where she acknowledged that she had forgotten how to just stop, in the midst of the busyness of her life, to just breathe and reflect.

Marie had difficulty imagining how her life could be different, especially with so many other things vying for her time and attention. We then talked about the 'mirror' exercise, only this time I asked her to imagine that the mirror had brought her forward into her future, by exactly one year. I asked her to abandon all the reasons that she thought would prevent her from achieving this future, and to just relax and let her imagination take charge. This turned out to be a powerful exercise for Marie, as it reconnected her to hopes that she had once dreamed of achieving, but had given up on for a variety of reasons, many of those being self imposed.

As a mother, with family as my top value, I can understand how the role of being a mum can blind us from creating a vision for our life, that also includes our passions, dreams and hopes. Being a parent is demanding, that's for sure, and it's is easy to feel undeserving as your children take priority. But it does not also mean the complete neglect of our individual needs and dreams. Marie had fallen into the trap of putting her life on hold, using the old age excuse of 'when'. Her previous attempts to lose weight were tempered with "when I feel less stressed" and her attempts at managing stress were "when I have more time."

As Marie became more practiced using the 'mirror' exercise, the more sure she became about the future she wanted to create. Rather than staying stuck in the merry-go-round of routine and demands, Marie was able to also get a glimpse of what could be a better future for her, if she was willing to accept personal responsibility for her happiness and take positive action.

With the use of the self-care wheel, we were also able to put together a plan of action, starting with the 'ABC' approach to her specific goals.

Paul

Paul is a 35 year old single professional male, with a past history of anxiety and depression. Having previously tried several other therapies and medication intervention, Paul still struggled significantly with anxiety, particularly social anxiety. He came to me for personal coaching, primarily to see if I could help him achieve the goal of attending a forthcoming family celebration. After much discussion, we agreed on a plan of action.

Paul agreed to try to turn his anxiety into action. His previous coping style was that of avoidance. This in turn not only fuelled his anxiety further, but caused him a great deal of regret and sadness. Paul also had developed the habit of 'compare and despair', and 'future-tripping,' which further added to his anxiety and negative self-evaluation.

Over the following weeks preceding the family event, Paul decided to remain in, rather than avoid, socially uncomfortable situations, to test his coping ability. He began a 'thought journal' and also began the practice of a one minute mindfulness meditation. Additionally, he integrated affirmations and a gratitude journal into his daily practice. Journaling had a extremely positive effect on Paul, as he began to understand how he had allowed himself become victimised by his thoughts, many of which, were fear based, as a result of his catastrophic thinking. Journaling automatically empowered him to see things more clearly and rationally. 'Pause for Breath,' allowed Paul to take a mental step back, during high times of anxiety thus reducing the debilitating effects of panic.

Over time and practice, Paul began to acknowledge that, should the worst case scenario happen, he would in fact cope. He began to somewhat accept that it was okay to feel the negative effects that anxiety brought, and learned new ways of coping instead. Paul still battles with the effects of social anxiety, however he has achieved much and has made significant progress, allowing him to enjoy social interactions to levels he had previously believed unattainable.

The power of achievement, regardless of how small, is a self-reinforcing process, and really does serve as a catalyst to keep forging ahead, especially during dark days of self-doubt and an ebbing motivation

Afterword

Personal empowerment is fundamental to overall wellbeing and happiness. That is why this book is structured around a set of key characteristics that already exist within us, and for which can be tapped into, if our goal is to experience a happier, healthier and more meaningful life.

I thought long and hard about the title of the book and arrived at a title that I feel captures the spirit of living. I believe to live life well, is to live it fully, never settling for less than the life that each of us are capable of living. I see our Mojo as that fuel that drives us to achieve that goal.

To 'Reclaim Your Mojo' is to reignite that spark of hope and self-belief - it's about rekindling an appetite to live fully, to take a chance, to inspire positive change and to forge your own path, so that you can leave a great footprint in the sands of time.

I see resilience as the fuel that refills our mojo tank. When I look back over my own life, my capacity to bounce back has made the real difference. That said, one should not confuse the fact that resilient people are always positive and never give up. They also feel the various emotions and frustrations that come with stresses, but rather than allow these emotions to disruptive their life for too long, they take personal responsibility and take positive action.

The concepts, within System Pause, draw on the five core attributes that is evident in all resilient people. A vital part of this system is the practice of mindfulness and the breathing technique, 'Pause for Breath.'

The regular practice of both promotes calmness, clarity and focus, and fosters general mental wellbeing, especially useful in our world where stress and anxiety have risen to an all time high.

I also believe, that now more than ever, people need to be 'inspired to do' rather than be 'told to do,' which is why I reference the achievements of ordinary people achieving extraordinary feats, along with the sharing of my own personal experiences throughout the book.

System Pause is essentially a reservoir of useful practical knowledge that can be referred to, time and time again – particularly when our mojo tank is running low. It is worth keeping in mind, that life is not a rehearsal - you can live it better, sometime in the future, or you can 'Reclaim Your Mojo' and start living today.

Wishing you the very best of you,

Emily Hurley-Wilkinson

RECLAIM YOUR MOJO

The A-Z Guide

Assert yourself and ask for what you want. Negotiate for change and tell someone how you feel. Stop saying Yes when you mean No.

Breathe and allow things to pass. Nothing is ever really permanent. Most things usually don't matter in the bigger picture of your life; affirm 'it is what it is.'

Cultivate an attitude of gratitude. There is always something to be grateful for.

Develop awareness of what is triggering stress and anxiety for you. Use a journal to record these moments. Writing things out helps to regain perspective and puts you back in control.

Embrace change and feel the fear; it's the best way to strengthen your coping ability.

Forgive often including yourself, its' the quickest way to inner peace and freedom.

Galvanise yourself into action with the ABC guide to goals.

Hydrate yourself daily by keeping a bottle of water to hand. Drinking fluids is crucial for staying healthy and maintaining energy.

Indulge in visualizations regularly. Cut out images, pictures, symbols that make you feel inspired and hopeful and keep them visually displayed.

Judge less, support more. We don't know what's really going on in other's lives.

Keep socially connected. Regardless of your situation, prioritise social participation.

Let go of seeking approval from others. Make self-approval a priority; start a self-validation journal and acknowledge your achievements and progress to date. When you regularly praise and acknowledge your own value, self-approval becomes a habit.

Move about daily and replenish your lungs with fresh air. Any activity can get our bodies feel good hormones into action.

Never take life too seriously. Life is to be enjoyed not endured. Your sense of humour is one of the most powerful tools that you can access anytime, anywhere.

Open your mind and consider other perspectives. Like two sides of a coin there is usually another way of seeing things.

Push yourself, no matter how you are feeling. Positive action is the ultimate cure for lifting the spirit and for those that feel stuck.

Question everything - Don't take others opinions as facts, do your own research.

Relax and unwind. There are 168 hours in each week, and you alone get to choose how to use those hours. It is life critical that you allocate time to relax and unwind, in order to buffer life's stresses and strains.

Smile frequently - It not only increases your charisma but it acts as an anti-depressant and mood lifter.

Talking is therapy, especially when you're feeling low. A problem shared is always a problem halved.

Understand first, before being understood. We are all guilty of jumping to conclusions.

Variety is the spice of life. Try doing something different that breaks your usual routine. Try out a new route to work, visit somewhere new, experiment with food, change your hairstyle or try out some new colours for your wardrobe.

Welcome change – most of us like to play it safe, but there are plenty of benefits to be had from stepping out of our comfort zone. Not only will your brain benefit but so too will your self-worth.

Xcel in all you do. You can only ever give it your best, be sure to give life the very best of you.

You are imperfectly perfect - embrace your uniqueness.

Zero in on the present moment. Being in the present moment naturally changes your emotional state to one of calm. Start up a one minute mindfulness meditation daily.

Inspired by my Dad

Lose Your Self-Doubt

Life is unpredictable, that much I know.

There will always be situations that will push us to a new low.

In times of adversity and days of unrest, be still and take comfort, you're doing your best.

No one is perfect, nor ever will they be, for perfection is a perception of things, we think we can see.

Comparisons are foolish – they lead us astray.

But by changing your attitude you can create a new day.

Life is for living, so get up and about.

Reclaim your Mojo and lose your self - doubt.

Copyright © Emily Hurley-Wilkinson

References

1. V. M. Lewis
2. John Allan Paulos
3. Karen Ravn
4. https://www.ted.com/talks/amy_cuddy_your_body_language_shapes_who_you_are
5. Vironika Tugaleva
6. Tsujimoto, M., Imura, S. & Kanda, H. Recovery and reproduction of an antarctic tardigrade retrieved from a moss sample frozen for over 30 years. Cryobiology 72, 78–81, doi:10.1016/j.cryobiol.2015.12.003 (2016).
7. Block JP, He Y, Zaslavsky AM, Ding L, Avanian JZ. Psychosocial stress and change in weight among US adults. Am J Epidemiol. 2009;170(2):181-192
8. Dr. Masaru Emoto, The Message from Water: The Message from Water is Telling Us to Take a Look at Ourselves. 1. Hado. 2000. ISBN 9784939098000
9. Chu Chin-Ning (Variation of)
10. Various
11. James N. Watkins
12. Various
13. Benjamin Franklin
14. Amish Proverb
15. Wayne Dyer
16. Elbert Hubbard
17. Nelson Mandela (Variation of)
18. Brian Tracy

19. Lao Tzu
20. Dr Phil McGraw
21. Anaise Nin

RECLAIM YOUR mojo

If you've been inspired to **Reclaim Your Mojo,** get in touch and let Emily know about it.

www.emilyhurleywilkinson.com

www.reclaimyourmojo.com

Printed in Great Britain
by Amazon